The Heart of
Being

The Heart of

Being

MORAL AND ETHICAL TEACHINGS
OF ZEN BUDDHISM

by John Daido Loori

Edited by Bonnie Myotai Treace
and Konrad Ryushin Marchaj

Foreword by Hakuyu Taizan Maezumi

Charles E. Tuttle Co., Inc.
Boston • Rutland, Vermont • Tokyo

Published by Charles E. Tuttle Company, Inc. of Rutland, Vermont, and Tokyo, Japan, with editorial offices at 153 Milk Street, Boston, Massachusetts 02109.

Portions of this work have been previously published in the quarterly journal *Mountain Record*.

Library of Congress Cataloging-in-Publication Data

Loori, John Daido.
   The heart of being : moral and ethical teachings of Zen Buddhism /
John Daido Loori ; edited by Bonnie Myotai Treace and Konrad
Ryushin Marchaj.
      p. cm.
   ISBN 0-8048-3078-9
   1. Religious life—Zen Buddhism. 2. Buddhist precepts. 3. Zen
Buddhism—Discipline. 4. Buddhist ethics. I. Treace, Bonnie
Myotai. II. Marchaj, Konrad Ryushin. III. Title.
   BQ9286.L66 1996
   294.3'5—dc20   96-25175
                                                        CIP

First edition
10 9 8 7 6 5 4 3 2 1
05 04 03 02 01 00 99 98 97 96

Cover design by Frances Kay
Printed in the United States of America

*Nine Bows in deep gratitude
to my late teacher
Master Hakuyu Taizan Maezumi
for revealing to me
the Heart of Being*

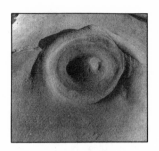

CONTENTS

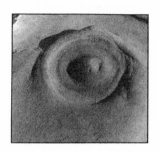

FOREWORD

Jukai: Receiving the Precepts

Author's Note: I originally hoped that my teacher, Maezumi Roshi, would write the foreword to this book. With his untimely death in May 1995, that became impossible. Still, I wanted to share some of his words. This teaching on the precepts was given by Roshi in the early 1980s. It is as alive now as it was then, and it provides an excellent entry point to this book.

*J*ukai literally means "to receive the *kai*, receive the precepts," but in a deeper sense *ju* is a synonym for *kaku*, "to realize." Buddha himself is called *kakusha*, "the realized or enlightened person," and *kai* does not merely mean "precept" as such; *kai* is a synonym of Buddha-nature. In other words, *jukai* means "to realize the Buddha-nature."

Another definition of jukai that I quote when we perform the jukai ceremony is "to truly realize what transmission means." In a sense, there is nothing to be transmitted; you have to realize your true self or Buddha-nature by yourself. The same thing is true of jukai: to truly receive the precepts is in itself to realize your true nature.

At the end of the jukai ceremony, I ask you three times, "Will you maintain the precepts well? Will you maintain them well? Will you *really* maintain them well?" And you answer, "Yes . . . yes . . . yes." We repeat it three times to make it really certain. At that moment, you are what we call *kai tai,* "the body of the kai." Buddha-nature is revealed in you. At the beginning of the ceremony we repeat the verse of *sange,* "repentance" or "atonement." But that repentance is not merely to repent for our wrongdoings. It is not that limited. We explain *sange* in three ways, which correspond to the three fundamental aspects of the Buddha Way: samadhi, precepts, and wisdom. The first aspect we call *shuso sange:* to penetrate deep into samadhi and see the Buddha; to realize who Buddha is. The next is called *saho sange,* which is closer to the usual understanding of repentance. We repent for whatever we did that was inadequate or wrong, and we cleanse ourselves—our body, mouth, and mind. And the third aspect is called *musho sange. Musho* literally means "no nature," which is a synonym of true nature, of Buddha-nature. To realize the Buddha-nature that transcends the dichotomies of good and bad, right and wrong, is repentance.

Shuso sange corresponds to samadhi. To really penetrate into samadhi and meet the Buddha, to see our true nature, is atonement. *Saho sange* corresponds to maintaining the precepts the best way that we can. Of course, the question What are the precepts? is a big matter in itself. Lastly, *musho sange* is equivalent to wisdom. It is to reveal the wisdom through which we see the true nature of ourselves that transcends good and bad, right and wrong.

In a sense, we can say that our atonement itself is the Buddha Treasure. Usually, we think that the Buddha was a prince who lived in India twenty-five hundred years ago, left his castle and family at the age of twenty-nine, and after six years of hard practice attained enlightenment. Of course, that is Buddha, too. But what Shakyamuni realized—the very nature of ourselves that is no-nature, the wisdom that we call *anuttara-samyaksambodhi*, the supreme, unsurpassable Way, the very best wisdom—we also call the Buddha Treasure of One Body. Of the Dharma Treasure of One Body, we say it is "pure and genuine, apart from defilements." The Dharma Treasure is also no-nature—that is why it is genuine. And because of that very no-nature, things appear to be as they are, not only ourselves, but all phenomenal existence. Everything is the result of causation, and causation in its very nature is no-nature. This no-nature is Buddha-nature—supreme wisdom, supreme Way, supreme enlightened state that is the Buddha Treasure. As we are, each one of us is distinctly different—that is the Dharma Treasure. All taken together as one is the Buddha Treasure. And the plain fact that these two are inseparable is called the Sangha Treasure. In other words, each one of us manifests as the Three Treasures. The Three Treasures are nothing but each one of us, the phenomenal world. To realize this is the true meaning of jukai.

We also have what we call the *realized* Three Treasures. The historical Buddha Shakyamuni who realized enlightenment is the realized Buddha Treasure. The content of that realization is the Dharma Treasure. Those who study the Buddha Way, the Buddha-dharma, as we are doing, are the Sangha Treasure.

To receive the Three Treasures means to identify ourselves with the reality that is our very life. The fundamental form and functioning of the Three Treasures, of our total existence, is the Three Pure Precepts and the Ten Grave Precepts. In other words, to receive the Pure Precepts and the Grave Precepts means to identify ourselves with the harmonious functioning of all life. When we receive the precepts, we are not given something that exists outside ourselves. In receiving the *kai* we reveal our life as the very body, form, and functioning of the enlightened state itself.

Gesshu Zenji, one of the outstanding Soto masters who lived in the seventeenth century, composed poems from time to time, and these poems were compiled into a book by one of his successors. The following poem is found in that collection:

> *Receiving the precepts,*
> > *sentient beings are one with*
> > > *Buddhas—*
> > *Buddhas are one with all beings.*
> *Individuals, just as they are,*
> > *reveal the unity of Buddhas and*
> > > *beings,*
> > *without inside or outside.*
> *It is wholly manifested*
> > *at this very moment,*
> > *in this very place.*

At the moment of receiving jukai, your very nature is revealed as the Three Treasures. That is why, in the jukai ceremony, we say: *Kie bukkyo; kie hokyo; kie sokyo.* "Being one with the Buddha, dharma, and sangha has been completed, has been accomplished." Receiving jukai, we confirm ourselves as being one with the Buddha, as children of the Buddha. We chant this at the end of jukai ceremony: "When all sentient beings receive the Buddhas' precepts, they enter the realm of the Buddhas, and their position is the same as that of the great enlightened person. Indeed, they are the children of the Buddhas." Their position is the same, yet they are as different from the Buddhas as children are from grown-ups. Of course, sooner or later each one of us grows up, but from the beginning we are all members of the Buddha family. To receive jukai is to reveal and affirm this wonderful truth.

—HAKUYU TAIZAN MAEZUMI

PREFACE

The temple bell has begun ringing, slow lolling strikes resonate throughout the monastery, calling the sangha together. It is the morning this spring's jukai, or precepts ceremony, will take place. Gray-robed students, family, visitors, and the resident monastics all enter the training hall as the bell speeds up, the space between the strikes growing smaller and smaller, the dynamic between sound and silence becoming charged. As the five students who will make their vows this day line up in the zendo, there is a palpable tenderness throughout the room. The gesture they are making is a gift for each person present, received as a kind of nourishment. So many of us arrive at Zen practice heart-starved and cynical that when there is a public reminder, like this ceremony, of the unbounded love that is Buddhism in practice, it can feel like the requiting of some unrecognized longing. A heart-to-heart, mind-to-mind transmission of truth: and so we celebrate.

This book by Abbot John Daido Loori presents the Buddhist precepts as a feast to nourish the deepest hungers of the human psyche. It is a presentation of not just the recipes—the descriptions of the external forms and ceremonies—but of the full-bodied process of searching, finding, cooking, tasting, digesting, giving strength, and serving others that the precepts invite. And it is as simple as it is grand. The irrational, unearned, singular beauty of the bell's sound, the vast silence and space that gives it definition. In taking up the moral and ethical teachings of Zen, we bring to our lips the morsel that nourishes all life; we vow to live in harmony with all beings, as well as to move with boldness and clarity to take care of life. The seeming paradoxes that may have provided a lifelong excuse for hesitancy and irresponsibility no longer serve as justifications for inaction. As Abbot Loori reminds his students in each jukai, responsibility for the "whole catastrophe" sits where we each sit, walks where we walk. The hands of great compassion get their wisdom and energy from how fully we realize and practice that responsibility.

The students bring their hands into *gassho*, identifying left with right, self with other, teacher with student. Each of them has walked his or her own crooked path to this moment. In the Mountains and Rivers Order founded by Abbot Loori, the requirements preliminary to jukai are a test of the students' commitment. They include at least one year of training as a formal student in the Order, a year of reading, studying, examining one's own life and the Buddhist precepts, engaging in intensive periods of zazen at a minimum of two complete sesshins, doing liturgical service positions, and attending the monthly *fusatsu* (renewal of vows) ceremonies. This culminates in a week of residential training with the teacher, with daily talks, question-and-answer periods, and one-to-one meetings in *dokusan* interspersed with zazen and the hand-sewing of a *rakusu*. The rakusu is pieced together from scraps of cloth joined as much by the black thread stitching through them as by the silent chanting that accompanies each poke and pull of the needle: "Being one with the Buddha; Being one with the dharma; Being one with the sangha." By week's end, the heart has become a raw place. The possibilities intrinsic to basing one's life motion in that still center—the heart of being—have become personal possibilities. This preliminary work enables a vow to form.

The work, as this book details, is deep and uncompromising in its thoroughness. The precepts deal with integrity—both as our inherent nature and the realization of our vows. It is unending, and sometimes hard work. The day prior to this jukai one of the students felt she should not be allowed to participate in the ceremony. When asked why, she tearfully reported, "You don't know me. I can be so awful." Her humility was answered with the fact that "*We* can all be so 'awful.' That's why the precepts are important. Please, serve the sangha your practice." Many of us indulge in the notion that we are so special in our insensitivity that we don't deserve another chance. To be nourished by the precepts is to get over our self-preoccupation and just practice. This student receives the precepts, the sangha gratefully receives her vow, and everyone is able to live a little more fully in reality. Opening up the process of receiving the precepts to those who will find this book in their hands is offered in the same spirit: that we may each hear the calling of the bell, live more fully in reality, and nourish one another with wisdom's complete confidence and compassion's tender and soothing hands.

—BONNIE MYOTAI TREACE

ACKNOWLEDGMENTS

The inspiration for this book came from the work on the precepts I did with my teacher, Taizan Maezumi Roshi, during the course of my training and from the ongoing precepts study that students at Zen Mountain Monastery undertake with me.

I am grateful to my successor, Bonnie Myotai Treace, and to Konrad Ryushin Marchaj for their editorial work on this volume. They aptly managed to take the spoken word and create a book that retains the spirit and the scope of my intent in the original discourses. Many thanks go to Desmond Gando Gilna and Janice Senju Baker for transcribing the talks that make up most of this volume, and to Geoffrey Shugen Arnold and Pat Jikyo George for invaluable input that helped clarify the overall structure of the chapters and eliminate redundancies. Vanessa Goddard assisted in the compilation of the glossary and the front matter of the book. A deep bow to all of them for their persistence and attentiveness to detail.

Finally, I would like to thank the students who, through many years of vigorously engaging the active edge of these moral and ethical teachings, helped me deepen and clarify my appreciation of the uniqueness and far-reaching implications of the Buddhist precepts.

PART I

Jukai:
The Ceremony of Precepts

·

INTRODUCTION

Right Action:
Giving Life to the Buddha

Most people who study Buddhism are familiar with the enlightenment teachings of Shakyamuni—the teachings of the Four Noble Truths, the doctrine of no-self, the principle of interdependent co-origination. Fewer people are aware that Shakyamuni also provided frequent, compelling teaching on a wide range of social and economic issues that impact the general welfare of all the life on our planet. He taught about government, politics, and the difficulties involved in mature citizenship and interpersonal relationships. That his teaching extends so dynamically into "right action" indicates that the Buddha's wisdom can be appreciated not just in monasteries but also on the streets and in the households of the twenty-first century. As we navigate the moral and ethical dilemmas of modern life, the Buddha's teaching can provide a way to see our way home. Indeed, the precepts of the Buddha can transform that navigation into something frankly wondrous: the life of the Buddha realized as our own life.

Being thoroughly educated and originally trained to become a ruler in his nation-state, Shakyamuni was exposed to the conflicts and problems arising in the social sphere. This made him acutely aware of the complexities of social conditions and their moral and ethical underpinnings. He was an extraordinary person by conventional standards. His enlightenment experience integrated his personality with a deep appreciation of the ground of being.

Following his enlightenment, he remained in the world teaching for forty-seven years, developing skillful means to respond to the searching questions of his students. He had plenty of opportunities to see how his teachings were manifesting and to correct, redirect, broaden, and focus them. During those forty-seven years, his teachings evolved to better and better meet the challenges his students were facing.

Because his experience as an astute social observer became interfused with his absolute wisdom, it is worthwhile to study his teachings about social and economic conditions in relation to spiritual practice and ethical life. Many of the Buddha's students were not drawn to the monastic way of life but remained in the world. Many of the dilemmas they encountered remain relevant today and will remain relevant as long as human nature exists. He had to address the life questions that were of burning concern to the people coming to his discourses; otherwise, they would not have been able to really hear him.

One of the central observations Buddha made about the breakdown of the social fabric is that poverty is the chief cause of immorality and crime. Theft, violence, hatred, cruelty, all result from poverty. It seems that ancient governments in India, like many governments today, tried to handle the problem of crime through punishment. They attempted to suppress it. Buddha said that attempts to control crime will ultimately be futile. This kind of control is like building a dam to hold back rising water. The barrier will hold back the water, but the barrier will always need to be there, and there will always be a threat of the water's spilling over or sweeping the dam away. Buddha said that if you want to eradicate crime, the economic conditions of the people have to be improved.

He encouraged people in businesses to provide adequate wages to their employees. He said that governments should make opportunities for everyone to be employed, for everyone to earn a sufficient income. When people are freed from their poverty, they rarely commit crimes born of desperation.

While Buddha championed improvement of economic conditions, he clearly differentiated this from hoarding wealth. He taught about "just a right amount" of wealth. There should be enough to sustain oneself, some savings, and plenty to share appropriately with others. He actually spelled out how much of the earnings one should save, how much to operate with, how much to reinvest in one's business, how much to give to people who are more needy. He did not just expound the lofty *dharma;* he also got nitty-gritty and pragmatic in his teachings. Sometimes he talked like a cave-dwelling sage, sometimes like a good bookkeeper.

In the context of the teachings of the Eightfold Path, Buddha helped householders by elaborating on the topic of right livelihood. Besides indicating what trades a person should avoid in order to actualize the innate harmony of this world, he spoke about the qualities one should cultivate in one's work. When a student asked for doctrines that would help in attaining happiness and peace in this lifetime, the Buddha listed four points pertaining to one's profession. First, one should be skilled, efficient, honest, and energetic in whatever profession one engages oneself. One should thoroughly master it. Second, one should protect one's income and savings, one's home, the fruits of one's efforts. Third, one should cultivate good friends— people who are honest, faithful, and open-minded, friends who reinforce the virtuous qualities of the dharma. Fourth, one should find the middle way in dealing with money: do not be extravagant, do not be self-abnegating.

Buddha also described four virtues that are conducive to happiness. A person should have faith and confidence in his or her moral, spiritual, and intellectual values. Each one of us should keep these values conscious; we should really know what they are. This is reflected in Zen training today when we make vows to keep the Buddhist precepts and when we periodically renew those vows, making our values conscious and public. The second virtue the Buddha spoke of is that people should abstain from destroying life, stealing, cheating and falsehood, adultery, and intoxicating drinks. (This particular list was a kind of abridged precepts package directed to nonmonastic practitioners.) I find especially interesting the focus the Buddha places on use of intoxicants, citing the dangers they pose, citing their potential to turn people's lives upside down. Further, a person should practice charity and generosity, without craving recognition or needing a payoff for good acts. People should also, he taught, strive to develop the wisdom that leads to a complete cessation of suffering.

On another occasion, while talking with a successful banker who was one of his disciples, Buddha offered him advice about circumstances associated with happiness. He pointed out that there are several types of contentment—the happiness associated with enjoyment of economic security and sufficient wealth that was acquired by just and righteous means; the happiness that comes from spending that wealth liberally on oneself, one's family, one's friends, and on meritorious deeds; the happiness of being free from debts; and the happiness of living a faultless and pure life, without committing evil in thoughts, words, or deeds—of not creating evil karma. Three of these four contentments are economic in nature, implying that the Buddha clearly saw that not all of his students were destined for the lifestyle of the monastic renunciate and that there was a vital spiritual teaching and practice involving householders.

Outside the sphere of personal finances and making a living, Buddha commented frequently on the pointlessness of war. It is clear that Buddhism does not advocate violence and that its intrinsic message is one of peace and harmony. Buddha not only taught nonviolence but even went into the battlefield to prevent a war. There was a conflict between the Shakyas and their neighbors the Kuhlahs. These two tribes were getting ready to fight over a border dispute that involved the water rights to the river that ran between the two lands. Buddha intervened and helped the parties reach a settlement. He accomplished this goal by making people see the incredible waste and pain involved in ending human lives through war.

Buddha was also acutely aware of corruption in government. He knew about the hunger for, and the addiction to, power, and the vanity, intrigue, and malice that could infect ministers and kings. He saw that when officials were corrupt and unjust, the whole country would fall into a state of economic and spiritual decline. In his teaching "The Ten Duties of the King," he establishes guidelines for an effective and just government. What he said about the duties of the king can easily be translated and applied as the duties of a president, a prime minister, the head of a union, the chief officer of a large corporation or a small business, a legislator, or a judge. It is applicable to that broad segment of society that wields power and in many ways controls the lives of its people. And since all of us, whether we like it or not, take up the koan of power, this teaching applies to each of us as we realize our responsibility to this great earth and to one another.

The first of the ten duties is to be liberal and generous in giving, to be charitable. A ruler should not be attached to the wealth accumulated through position. Rather, it should be given away for the benefit and well-being of all people. Second, a ruler should be of high moral character and follow the precepts. Third, a ruler should be ready to sacrifice everything for the good of the people. He or she must be prepared to give up personal comfort, status and fame, even life itself, in the interest of those being served. This is a pretty extraordinary teaching. What would it be like if the highly visible figures in the life of a nation started to set examples of moderation and humility rather than excessiveness and arrogance? What would a model of such high moral standards do for a nation?

The fourth duty of a ruler is honesty and integrity. A ruler must be free of fear and favor in discharging the duties of office. There must be sincerity of intention and a commitment not to deceive the public. Fifth, a ruler must manifest kindness and gentleness, and possess a genial temperament. Sixth, a ruler should enjoy austerity in personal habits, leading a simple life and not indulging in luxuries, exercising self-control. Seventh, a ruler must bear no grudges and be free from hatred or ill-will.

The eighth duty is to actualize nonviolence, which means not only avoiding harming anyone but also actively promoting peace, preventing war, and opposing any activity that involves violence and destruction of life. Ninth, a ruler must practice patience, forbearance, tolerance, and understanding and be able to bear hardships, difficulties, and insults without becoming angry. The last duty is nonopposition, or nonobstruction. The ruler should not oppose the will of the people but should be in harmony with the welfare of all.

These guidelines actually became embodied in one political leader, King Ashoka of India, during the third century B.C.E. Ashoka's father and grandfather wished to conquer the whole Indian peninsula. When Ashoka came into power, he followed in their footsteps and continued the bloody conquest of the lands. He was directly responsible for the deaths of thousands of people.

Then something shifted. Ashoka changed. He took Buddhist vows and publicly expressed his repentance. He atoned and declared that he would never draw his sword for any reason. He vowed to devote his life to nonviolence. He entered the practice path of mindfulness, self-control, serenity, and wisdom. Not only did he renounce war, he also established a government that for three hundred years would have no need to exercise force in instituting laws. Education flourished, health care improved dramatically. Ashoka's history is especially remarkable because all of these changes occurred at the zenith of his power. He could easily have continued his campaign. Yet he saw something, something about the true nature of power, that made him renounce war and violence and turn to peace and nonviolence. If this shift happened once, it can happen again.

It is also fascinating in Ashoka's case that the bordering countries did not take advantage of his pacifism. They did not attack. There were no internal revolts within the empire. His was a very peaceful and enduring reign.

The moral and ethical teachings of the Buddha have been around for twenty-five hundred years, yet even among Buddhists there are very few who are aware of their existence, much less their application. In these days when the breakdown of social values and a general discontentment with our way of life is so distressing to so many, the Buddha's teachings are an especially important gift that Buddhist practitioners can bring to the West.

Because of the extent and accessibility of all types of communication, there is a window of opportunity open to make this wisdom available to a great number of people. It can be communicated in ways that are accessible and relevant. Most important, though, Buddhist practitioners must take responsibility for manifesting these teachings in their lives and must recognize their manifestation in others' lives as well.

All of the Buddha's teachings are really none other than the precepts: the vow to give life to the Buddha, to return to the heart of being. Any time we renew our precept vows, we renew our ability to practice them more vigorously. Practicing them does not mean never violating them. It means practicing them, and like practicing the breath, we are always starting new, starting fresh. This is right action. When you practice the precepts, you create an energy around you that is palpable to others.

This practice is contagious. *Zazen* is contagious.

Living the precepts is contagious. Realizing the ground of being and actualizing it in our lives is contagious. Your practice transforms not only you but all those who come in contact with you. We have a wonderful gift at our disposal in these teachings of the Buddha; we should vow together that this gift will continue to heal and nourish all beings for countless generations to come. In making that vow, we realize the Buddha's precepts, we realize the heart of being as our own heart, the heart of all beings.

CHAPTER 1

Sacred Space:
The Heart of Being

Traditionally when people wanted to receive the precepts, they would gather at the temple on a Buddhist holiday and together go before a teacher to make a formal request in a public ceremony. I find it to be much more intimate when students approach me one-on-one in *dokusan* and ask to receive this extraordinary teaching. It gives me an opportunity to find out why they want to take this step and to determine whether the time is right. It is the beginning of a commitment to work together on the precepts, so it needs to be personal. Why is it important to them? What does making a commitment to practice the precepts mean to them?

Unfortunately, many people see the *rakusu* received during the precepts ceremony as a kind of status symbol. I once had a student interested in receiving the precepts tell me that it made him feel more important than the other students. It is imperative to understand that taking the Buddhist precepts and wearing a rakusu makes us the servants of other people, not superior to them. Our vow is to be a servant to all sentient beings. We are at their disposal to help them do what they need to do. To me, wearing a rakusu means living the life of a Buddha, manifesting our lives as Buddhas. Buddhas do not put themselves above anything. In Buddha there is no separation. To be Buddha is to not separate yourself from others anytime, anyplace.

There are certain aspects of the precepts that are not dealt with publicly. One of the reasons for this apparent caution is that in order for the teachings to be heard, a particular state of consciousness needs to be present. I can talk about the precepts at any stage of a student's training, but in the beginning the precepts are usually grasped only intellectually. This can lead to misunderstanding and misinterpretation. When this happens, the precepts cease to function the way they were originally intended.

In order to keep my own vow as a teacher, I like to wait until a student demonstrates a certain maturity of practice before I agree to his or her petition to receive the precepts. If you examine it closely, you will see that in any field of endeavor, there is a level of maturity that needs to exist before communication is possible. You may enjoy music very much, and you can listen to a very fine violinist, but you will hear it differently if you are a student of the violin. The more experienced and mature you become in your playing, the more sensitive you will become to the nuances previously hidden to you.

It's like being in the wilderness. We may enjoy being in the woods, in nature, but how aware are we of what goes on in the forest—the sounds, the tracks that cross our path, the smells that are in the air? How much does the forest really communicate? You will find that the more time you spend there, the more you immerse yourself in it, the more mature a person of the woods you will become, and the more aware you will become of what the woods have to teach, to communicate.

When a student has completed the preliminary training with a teacher of the precepts, we do a precepts ceremony known as *jukai*. Students now make their vows public, receive the precepts into their lives, and be supported by the larger community as they take up the challenges and responsibilities of being a Buddhist. This book is an invitation to be part of the ceremony of jukai, and it surveys many of the elements of what is experienced by those participating. In this ceremony, as in many Buddhist ceremonies, a sacred space is first created. The officiant of the ceremony enters the hall before anyone else and dedicates the room; here at Zen Mountain Monastery we use a small pine branch and water from the mountain spring to asperge the room. The large main bell then begins to sound, calling everyone together for jukai. The hall fills with family, friends, and practitioners who will witness the morning's events.

The main altar of the room is closed, and a new altar is established at the spot midroom where the precepts ceremony is to be held. The preceptor, or *kaishi*, teacher of the precepts, takes the position of the Buddha in this new altar. In a sense, it is the Buddha who will give the precepts to the recipients. The new altar contains everything that the main altar contains, and each of the recipients faces that altar in the process of receiving the precepts. That confrontation is a meeting of the heart/mind of the student with the heart/mind of the Buddha: it requires a very honest, bare willingness to see into oneself.

For much of the ceremony the recipients' hands

remain in *gassho,* palms together. The gassho is called "the pure mudra of the three karmas: body, mouth, and mind." Because all Buddhas are said to emerge from this mudra, it is sometimes called the Mother Mudra. The left hand and the right hand, all the dualities—absolute and relative, good and bad, up and down, self and other—are brought together in this one reality. The simple gesture of gassho is an acknowledgment of this essential unity, finding its expression in this body, this mind, this time.

The instructions for gassho say, "Do not cross your fingers, do not allow space between your hands, and do not fix your elbows or arms against your body. Look at your fingertips and concentrate, making body and mind quiet, focused, and calm." Needless to say, if we did that every time we brought our hands palm to palm in gassho, that gassho would have an incredible impact not only on our life but on all the life we gassho to, sentient or insentient. The interpenetration and intermingling of all dualities is just this gassho.

The gassho combined with a standing bow is considered an informal bow. A more profound gesture is the full bow, or prostration. As the jukai ceremony begins, each participant makes a series of full prostrations. First, we do a full bow to the Buddha. In that prostration we completely identify with Shakyamuni. In other words, the separation, the gap, is closed, and Buddha and self become one reality, just as when we bow to one another.

Then the recipients do a full bow in the direction in which their parents live or are buried. If their parents have come to the ceremony, the students go to where the parents are seated in the *zendo* and prostrate at their feet. This bow is a way of acknowledging and identifying with our own genetic lineage. Whether we like it or not, this is a part of who we are, our physical reality, and we should be who we are with no reservation whatsoever. It is with gratitude that we bow to our parents, and to their parents, back through successive generations, as well as to the Buddha. This is because in the ceremony of receiving the precepts—indeed, in any Buddhist ceremony—those are the things that are coming together: our genetic lineage and the lineage of the Buddhas and ancestors. They come together in us, and when we identify with them, we close the circle.

A third full bow is then made to the preceptor, the *kaishi*, representing the lineage of ancestors who have been handing down the precepts, mind-to-mind, from generation to generation, down to this time and this place. In bowing we are acknowledging all that is making it possible for us to receive these precepts. When each of these bows is done with an aware mind, an open mind, there is a sense of identification, unity, interpenetration, intermingling. There is a wholeness to our reality.

During the ceremony the preceptor dips the pine sprig into the water, touches the dripping pine to his own head, returns the water back into the cup, and then asperges the head of the student. This is a gesture of the mind-to-mind connectedness between the teacher and the student. In this part of the ceremony, the preceptor chants several different *dharanis*, sacred incantations. There are *dharanis* for eliminating disasters and for clarity and purification. The preceptor also uses different mudras—protective mudras, purification mudras, and mudras that invoke the Three Treasures.

Next the water is asperged to the right. This is for the four benevolences: our parents, our teachers, the nation, and the earth itself. Then the water is asperged to the left, and that is directed to all beings throughout space and time. In a sense, we can say that the same inclusiveness is reflected when we gassho. Everybody is included—nobody is left out. In this way the ceremony is not just between the preceptor and the recipient but includes the entire community, or *sangha*.

Recipients vow to keep each of the precepts, to live their life in accord with the precepts, to practice and return to the precepts when they become lost. In the ceremony, each recipient vows and makes a bow as each of the precepts is given. After the ceremony has been completed, the preceptor chants the Gatha on Receiving the Precepts. The *gatha* says, "When sentient beings receive the *shila* [precepts], they enter the realm of Buddhas." What is the realm of the Buddhas? When the precepts are truly received, when the student's heart is open and receptive, then the heart of the student and the heart of the Buddha become one reality. The precepts are the definition of the life of a Buddha. This is the way a Buddha lives his or her life. Each step of the process is about identifying with that interpenetration, that sense of unity.

The gatha continues, "When sentient beings receive the *shila,* they enter the realm of the Buddhas, which is none other than the great enlightenment." *Anuttara-samyaksambodhi* is the great enlightenment. It is none other than the life of all sentient beings, my life and your life, and the lives of all the ancestors who have passed the teaching down. But to understand or believe that fact is quite different from realizing it.

The last line of the gatha says, "Truly they are the children of the Buddha." This means that those who receive the precepts are the offspring of that life called Buddha. *Buddha* literally means enlightened one, and it also refers to Shakyamuni Buddha. When one truly receives the precepts, not just listens to them but really receives them with the whole body and mind, then the life of the Buddha is born in that moment. That is what it means to give life to the Buddha. That is what it means to realize the heart of being. This is a hard thing to communicate in this day and age, because so much of what we do when we interact is by its very nature superficial. We rarely get into the depths of our being. We have a tendency to go through the gestures and the movements, with a kind of monkey-see, monkey-do attitude toward spiritual practice. It is very easy to take that habit into a ceremony as profound as jukai and miss what is going on. But the possibility always exists of making it real. Even if it does not happen before or during the ceremony, the opportunity is always there to make it real. The way we make it real is with our mind.

At the heart of the precepts ceremony, at the heart of any ceremony—indeed, at the heart of being itself—is what Bodhidharma calls "the beholding mind." This is the mind that has insight. It involves a kind of seeing that is different from looking, a seeing that involves whole body-and-mind intimacy. This is the aware and conscious mind, which must be brought forth in order to give life to the precepts and manifest the heart of being in one's own life.

CHAPTER 2

Kyojukaimon:
Commentary on Master Dogen's Teachings on the Precepts

The "Kyojukaimon: Instructions Given on the Shila" is Master Dogen's teachings on the precepts as received from his teacher Ju-ching in China. My teacher passed it on to me as part of his teaching; I pass it on to my students as follows:

The great precepts of the Buddhas are maintained carefully by all Buddhas. Buddhas give them to Buddhas. Ancestors give them to ancestors. Receiving the precepts goes beyond past, present, and future. Practice is a continuum. Realization is a continuum. It exists from ancient times to the present and into the future. The great master Shakyamuni Buddha transmitted the precepts to Mahakashyapa, and Mahakashyapa transmitted them to Ananda. Thus they have been transmitted generation after generation, down to me, in the eightieth generation. Now I, as head priest of Zen Mountain Monastery, give them to you in order to express my gratitude for the compassionate benevolence of the Buddhas and thus make them the eyes of all sentient beings. Indeed, this is the way to practice and maintain the living wisdom of the Buddhas. May the wisdom and compassion of all Buddhas and ancestors guide and verify this action.

First, you must make atonement and take refuge in the precepts, as follows:

> *All evil karma ever committed by me since of old,*
> *Because of my beginningless greed, anger, and*
>   *ignorance,*
> *Born of my body, mouth, and thought,*
> *Now I atone for it all.*

With the guidance of the teachings of the Buddhas and ancestors, we have discarded and purified all karma of body, mouth, and thought and have attained great immaculateness by the power of atonement.

Next you should take refuge in the Three Treasures: the Buddha, the Dharma, and the Sangha. The Three Treasures have three aspects, called the One-Body Three Treasures, the Realized Three Treasures, and the Maintained Three Treasures.

Anuttara-samyaksambodhi is called the Buddha Treasure. Being pure and genuine, apart from the dust, is the Dharma Treasure. The virtues and merits of harmony are the Sangha Treasure. These are the One-Body Three Treasures.

To realize and actualize *bodhi* is called the Buddha Treasure. The realization of the Buddha is the Dharma Treasure. To penetrate into the Buddha-dharma is the Sangha Treasure. These are the Realized Three Treasures.

Guiding the heavens and guiding the people, sometimes appearing in vast emptiness, sometimes appearing in a speck of dust, is the Buddha Treasure. Revolving in the sutras and the oceanic storehouse, guiding inanimate things and guiding animate beings, is the Dharma Treasure. Freed from all suffering and liberated from the house of the three worlds is the Sangha Treasure. These are the Maintained Three Treasures.

When you take refuge in the Buddha, the Dharma, and the Sangha, you obtain the great precepts of all Buddhas. Make the Buddha your teacher, and do not follow deluded ways.

Next are the Three Pure Precepts.

The first pure precept is *Not creating evil.*

"This is the abiding place of all Buddhas. This is the very source of all Buddhas."

The second pure precept is *Practicing good.*

"This is the dharma of *samyak-sambodhi.* This is the way of all beings."

The third pure precept is *Actualizing good for others.*

"This is to transcend the profane and to be beyond the holy. This is to liberate oneself and others."

These are called the Three Pure Precepts.

Next are the Ten Grave Precepts.

The first grave precept is *Affirm life; do not kill.*

"Life is nonkilling. The seed of Buddha grows continuously. Maintain the wisdom life of Buddha, and do not kill life."

The second grave precept is *Be giving; do not steal.*

"The mind and externals are just thus. The gate of liberation is open."

The third grave precept is *Honor the body; do not misuse sexuality.*

"The three wheels—body, mouth, and mind; greed, anger, and ignorance—are pure and clean. Nothing is desired. Go the same way as the Buddha."

The fourth grave precept is *Manifest truth; do not lie.*

"The dharma wheel unceasingly turns, and there is neither excess nor lack. Sweet dew permeates the universe. Gain the essence and realize the truth."

The fifth grave precept is *Proceed clearly; do not cloud the mind.*

"'It' has never been. Do not be defiled. 'It' is indeed the great clarity."

The sixth grave precept is *See the perfection; do not speak of others' errors and faults.*

"In the midst of the Buddha-dharma, we are the same Way, the same dharma, the same realization, and the same practice. Do not speak of others' errors and faults. Do not destroy the Way."

The seventh grave precept is *Realize self and other as one; do not elevate the self and blame others.*

"Buddhas and ancestors realize the absolute emptiness and realize the great earth. When the great body is manifested, there is neither outside nor inside. When the dharma body is manifested, there is not even a single square inch of earth upon which to stand."

The eighth grave precept is *Give generously; do not be withholding.*

"One phrase, one verse, ten thousand forms, one hundred grasses, one dharma, one realization, all Buddhas, all ancestors. Since the beginning, there never has been withholding."

The ninth grave precept is *Actualize harmony; do not be angry.*

"It is not regressing, it is not advancing. It is not real, it is not unreal. There is an illuminated cloud ocean, there is an ornamented cloud ocean."

The tenth grave precept is *Experience the intimacy of things; do not defile the Three Treasures.*

"Living the dharma with the whole body and mind is the heart of wisdom and compassion. All virtues return to the ocean of reality. You should not comment on them; just practice them, realize them, and actualize them."

The moral and ethical teachings of the Buddha are thus. Practice them well and give life to the Buddha.

There are other translations of this teaching of Dogen. Some are quite different. This translation comes closest to the way we understand, practice, and teach the precepts at Zen Mountain Monastery.

Many people have asked why it is necessary to formally take the precepts. At one point in my training, that was my question, too. I felt that the precepts were already the guidelines to my life and that it was not necessary for me to say aloud, "I won't kill," because that was already my commitment. I did not understand why there needed to be a ceremony. To truly appreciate jukai, the precepts ceremony, we must keep in mind that it is one thing to make a vow to yourself and quite another to make a public vow. Somehow, when you make a vow public, it becomes much more conscious.

In order to practice the precepts, we need to be aware of them as our own vows. In the process of taking jukai, we should really make the precepts our own, viewing them not as something imposed from the outside, something restricting our life, but rather as a doorway to freedom. They are not meant to bind. They are not meant to limit. They are meant to liberate us. What binds us are the three poisons of greed, anger, and ignorance. What the precepts are about is wisdom, compassion, and realization—the other side of the three poisons.

To practice the precepts is to be in harmony with your life and with the universe. To practice the precepts means to be very conscious of what they are about and to be deeply honest with yourself. When you become aware of having violated a precept, just acknowledge that fact. Acknowledgment means taking responsibility, and that plays a key role in our practice. If you do not practice taking responsibility, you are not practicing. That is what is going on when you work with your breath in zazen. As your mind drifts off, you become aware of it. Acknowledge that fact and take responsibility for it; let it go and come back again to the breath. There is nobody but you involved in that process. There is nobody checking on whether you are letting go of thoughts or sticking with thoughts. So, it has to do only with you and your own integrity, being honest with yourself about your practice. In the silence of your own zazen, only you know whether you are diligently practicing.

It is the same with the precepts. Only you know when you have actually violated a precept, and only you can be at one with that violation. To be at one with it means to take responsibility. To take responsibility is to acknowledge yourself as master of your life. To take responsibility empowers you to do something about whatever it is that is hindering you. As long as we blame, as long as we avoid or deny, we remove from the realm of possibility the power to do something about our lives. We become totally dependent upon the ups and downs we create around us. There is no reason we should be subjected to anything when we have the power to see that we are the creator of everything. To acknowledge that simple fact is to take possession of the precepts, to make them our own, to give life to the Buddha.

Master Dogen said, "Practice and enlightenment are one." What that means is that zazen, the process undertaken to reach enlightenment, and enlightenment itself are

the same thing. When you sit, you manifest the enlightenment of all Buddhas. You actualize wisdom and compassion in the sitting itself. The same can be said for the
precepts—the precepts are the definition of the life of a
Buddha. They describe the way a Buddha lives his or her
life. Buddha and precepts are not two separate entities. To
practice the precepts is to manifest the wisdom and compassion of the Tathagata, the enlightened one.

When the dharma began to take root in this country,
numerous books appeared and many dilettantes became
involved in the practice. During those early years, there
arose a misconception about the role of morality and
ethics in the practice of the Buddha-dharma. Statements
that Zen was "beyond morality" were made by some dis-
tinguished writers, such as D. T. Suzuki, and people
assumed that this was correct. Nothing can be further
from the truth. Enlightenment and morality are one.
Enlightenment without morality is not true enlightenment. Morality without enlightenment is not complete
morality.

Zen is not beyond morality but a practice that takes
place within the world, based on a moral and ethical
teaching. This moral and ethical teaching has been
handed down with the transmission from generation to
generation. Unfortunately, not only did this seed of misconception find its way into print, but also no one both-
ered to correct it. For twenty years it went uncorrected,
and although there have been many teachers and many
books on Zen, few even attempt to address the subject.
Somehow, teachers in the East and West have tended to
shy away from writing about the precepts, perhaps fear-
ing being categorized as moralists.

At Zen Mountain Monastery the moral and ethical
teachings are one of the eight areas of training. The precepts

are not taken once in your practice and then forgotten. They are taught and practiced as part of our ongoing training. Before people receive the precepts, they are informed about and trained in what the precepts are.

In some centers, to receive the precepts means simply to do the ceremony. In other places there is not even a ceremony. Students are just handed rakusus to hang around their necks. At Zen Mountain Monastery, before students can receive the precepts they engage in a full year of preparation and then a week of intensive training, one-on-one with the teacher. From that point on, every time the rakusu appears around the neck of a student in the dokusan room, it is a sign of commitment—commitment to the lineage, to the sixteen precepts, to the teacher. That commitment provides an opportunity to explore the moral and ethical teachings as they appear in koans and in the daily life of the practitioner.

The precepts not only are being practiced by the students in their encounters in the world but are also coming up in the encounters with the teacher. By the time a student has come near to completing the koan study and is about to begin work on the 120 precepts koans, a solid foundation has been prepared.

There are thousands of Zen practitioners in our country. Hundreds of those who have received the precepts do not know what they have done. They have no idea what it means to take the precepts. Ask someone who has become a Buddhist and received the precepts what it means to take refuge in the Three Treasures. Ask yourself! What is refuge? What are the Three Treasures? We say, "Buddha, Dharma, and Sangha," but what does that mean? Those are the words. What is the essence of being one with the Buddha, being one with the Dharma, being one with the Sangha? It is not some idea. It is a living reality, a state of consciousness. It is a state of being in harmony with the moral and ethical teachings.

We live at a time of considerable moral crisis, as individuals, as a nation, and as a planet. The injury we do to one another, and to our environment, can be healed only by sound moral and ethical commitment. That does not mean being puritanical. It does not mean being moralistic. The precepts have a vitality different from any ethical teachings I have encountered in the great religions of the world. They are alive. They are not fixed. They are not a list of "dos and don'ts." They function broadly and deeply. They are based on interpenetration, co-origination, and the interdependence of all the aspects of the universe.

As you explore the precepts in your own life and come up with problems, bring those questions to dokusan as koans, and I will be happy to teach you. The precepts are incredibly profound. Do not take them lightly. Press against their edges. Push them. See where they take you. They manifest in ten directions. They are direct and challenging, yet subtle. Please use them. You are free to use the precepts, whether you have formally received them or not, whether you intend to receive them or not. When you have been using them and you feel they are a part of your life, when you are at ease working with them, then the precepts have been transmitted and received. That is the time to do the ceremony. So, please, take them. Make them your own. They are no small thing by any measure. They nourish, they heal, and they are the manifestation of compassion in a troubled world.

CHAPTER 3

Invocation:
Practicing Buddha

There are a number of questions I repeatedly hear from Zen students: What can I do about anger? How do I deal with envy and neediness? How can I practice when I feel impatient? The standard and dependable answer is, Let go. Usually, the question that comes back is, How do I let go? And the response to that is, Be the barrier that you are struggling with; experience the reality of no separation. This sounds like a simple enough formula, and it is. And it is probably because of that simplicity that it is so difficult to realize.

In order to appreciate in some depth the teachings of the nondual dharma, it is helpful to look at the karma of invocation, the karma of vow, and the karma of practice. Karma is activity itself, the process of cause and effect. Greed, anger, confusion, envy—all of the unwholesome conditions that we struggle to eliminate—are essentially our own karma. They did not just materialize out of the blue sky. They are not something that happens to you. They are something you do. What you do and what happens to you are the same thing.

Karma is blind to discrimination; it knows only the impartial force to propagate itself. Whatever you call good action results in good karma, whatever your reference system is. Whatever you call evil action results in evil consequences. Karma knows nothing about good and evil, it just ensures that the chain of cause and effect continues.

Many Buddhist ceremonies begin with an invocation. An accepted definition of invocation is a petition for help or support. To invoke is to call forth by incantation, to conjure spirits, to put into effect or operation, to bring about or cause. This is according to Webster's dictionary. Most of it fits a theistic framework fine but does not seem to apply to a nontheistic religion. We must look beyond definitions to see what is going on when we are invoking in Buddhism. What is the invoking about and how is it done?

Invocation has penetrating consequences. Let's look at body, mouth, and thought during invocation. What's going on when we invoke? In the jukai ceremony we invoke the Three Treasures, Shakyamuni Buddha, various bodhisattvas, and the lineage of the great teachers who passed on this tradition. We chant their names. We kneel and place our hands in gassho, expressing the unity of all dualities. We say, "Be one with the Buddha in the ten directions. Be one with the Dharma in the ten directions. Be one with the Sangha in the ten directions." And our mind is focused on that.

The body language of "being one with the Buddha" is very different from the body language of separation, of greed, anger, and ignorance. Body language always reflects what is going on inside. Our emotions and attitudes are clearly telegraphed, no matter how much we try to cover them up. Body attitude also affects our state of consciousness. A person who is sitting in a half-lotus posture with the hands in a cosmic mudra is in a very different state of consciousness from someone who is sitting hunched over in a chair, supporting chin on fist like Rodin's *The Thinker*.

Body posture alone creates a particular activity in the mind. Sitting like a Buddha is creating a Buddha. It is creating acceptance and touching the still point that is the life of each one of us. What our bodies are doing, what our voices are expressing, what our minds are experiencing, is precisely the karma that we are creating.

To appreciate the Buddhist way of understanding reality, it is paramount to understand how the mind functions. What we call reality, the totality of human experience, comes from the interaction of the organs of perception, an object or an event in the material world, and consciousness. Eye, ear, nose, tongue, body, and mind are organs of perception. When those six organs of perception come in contact with their respective objects, such as form, sound, or taste, that meeting point, along with consciousness, creates the human experience.

Remember that mind is an organ of perception, and thought is the object of that organ of perception. What form is to eye, thought is to mind. Mind, thought, and consciousness create reality. It is for that reason that in Buddhism a dream is considered as real as the reality we experience right now. From another perspective, the reality constructed by our waking consciousness is an illusion created by the senses.

When the self is forgotten there is no eye, ear, nose,

tongue, body, and mind. There is no form, sound, smell, taste, touch, or phenomenon. To forget the self is to realize the absolute basis of all the mental constructions. But as long as we are dealing with the eye, ear, nose, tongue, body, and mind, we are dealing in the world of phenomena, the world of dualities. And in the world of dualities we know very well what creates pain and suffering. We don't need any special education to comprehend it. We know what hurts us and hurts others. We know what anger is and what joy is. We know what turmoil is and what peace is. As Buddhists we should understand how we create these realities. Our experiences don't just happen to us. They also have to do with what we do.

That relationship between the mind's activity and karma was precisely elucidated by Bodhidharma in his sermons. A monastic once asked Bodhidharma: *The sutras say that someone who wholeheartedly invokes the Buddha is sure to be reborn in the Western Paradise. Since this door leads to Buddhahood, why seek liberation in beholding the mind?* Bodhidharma replied as follows: *If you are going to invoke the Buddha, you have to do it right. Unless you understand what invoking means, you'll do it wrong. And if you do it wrong, you'll never get anywhere. Buddha means awareness—the awareness of the body and the mind that prevents evil from arising in either. And to invoke means to call to mind, to call constantly to mind that which is being invoked and to follow it with all your might.*

This is what's meant by invoking. Invoking has to do with thought, not with language. If you use a trap to catch a fish, once you've succeeded you can forget the trap. And if you use language to find meaning, once you find it, you can forget language. To invoke the Buddha's name, you have to understand the dharma of invoking. If it's not present in your mind, your mouth chants an empty name. As long as you're troubled by the three poisons, by thoughts of yourself, deluded mind will keep you from seeing the Buddha and you'll only waste your effort.

Chanting and invoking are worlds apart. Chanting is done with the mouth; invoking is done with the mind. And because invoking comes from the mind, it is called a door to awareness. Chanting is centered in the mouth and appears as sound. If you cling to appearances while searching for meaning, you won't find a thing. Thus, the sages of the past cultivated introspection and not speech. This mind is the source of all virtues, and this mind is the chief of all powers.

The eternal bliss of nirvana comes from the mind at rest; rebirth and the three realms also come from the mind. The mind is the door to every world, and the world is the ford to the other shore. Those who know where the door is don't worry about reaching it. Those who know where the ford is don't worry about crossing it.

The people I meet nowadays are superficial. They think of merit as something that has form. They squander their wealth and butcher creatures of land and sea. They foolishly concern themselves with erecting statues and stupas, telling people to pile up lumber and bricks and to paint this blue and that green. They strain the body and mind, injure themselves, and mislead others. And they don't know enough to be ashamed. How will they ever become enlightened?

If you can simply concentrate your mind's inner light and behold its outer illumination, you'll dispel the three poisons and drive away the six thieves once and for all. And without effort you'll gain possession of an infinite number of virtues, perfections, and doors to the truth. Seeing through the mundane and witnessing the *sublime is less than an eye blink away. Realization is now. Why worry about gray hair? The true door is hidden and can't be revealed.*

When the first action is invocation, the karma that follows flows from that invocation. In the jukai ceremony we invoke, "Be one with the Buddha in the ten directions." When we say "the ten directions," we mean the whole phenomenal universe, reaching everywhere. The universe is vast and boundless, it has no edges. In invocation we identify with the boundlessness as well as with the historical Buddha. We invoke the Dharma, the teachings of the Buddha regarding our identity with all things. The teachings of the Buddha occupy the ten directions, the whole catastrophe. We then call to mind our identity with the sangha, the practitioners of the Buddhist dharma. Sangha is also all sentient beings. To be one with the Sangha is to be one with all sentient beings.

"Be one with the original teacher, Shakyamuni Buddha." "Be one with the compassionate Avalokiteshvara Bodhisattva, the goddess of compassion." How can you be one with compassion? "Be one with the great wise Samantabhadra Bodhisattva," another bodhisattva of compassion. We invoke Manjushri Bodhisattva, the bodhisattva of wisdom. We invoke Koso Joyo Daishi, Dogen Zenji; and Taiso Josai Daishi, Keizan Zenji—the founders of our lineage in Japan. "Be one with the successive great ancestors." What we are invoking are the Three Treasures, Shakyamuni Buddha, wisdom, compassion, the lineage of the ancestors. What is all of that? It is this very body and mind, and the body and mind of all beings. This is the teaching of the Buddha. It is the basis of the precepts and the basis of their activity in the world of differences.

When the first action is vow, we create the karma of

that vow. A vow is "a solemn promise or assertion, one by which people bind themselves to an act, service, or condition." When the first cause springs from enlightenment, all subsequent causes and effects are enlightened. "Sentient beings are numberless. I vow to save them." That vow is powerful. It is the declaration of our intent. It is our activity and karma. It will propagate itself, just like evil propagates itself. It is at this moment, the moment of the vow, that we can turn things around.

All this very naturally brings us to the karma of practice. Practice is actual performance or action. Practice is doing, carrying out tasks, applying one's energy. It is different from vowing, different from invoking. It is doing. Master Dogen taught: *All Buddhas always maintained dignified activity. This is practicing Buddha. Practicing Buddha is not the reward body of the Buddha and it's not the transformation body of the Buddha, either. It is not the self-enlightened body of the Buddha nor is it the enlightened body of other Buddhas. It is not acquired enlightenment. It is not innate enlightenment, not the nature of enlightenment, and not no enlightenment. None of these Buddhas are equal to practicing Buddha.*

We should know that all the Buddhas within the Buddha Way never expect enlightenment. The continuous development of Buddha occurs only through practicing Buddha. Those who believe that Buddha is self-awakening cannot even dream of practicing Buddha. In practicing, Buddha dignity is actualized from start to finish. That dignity appears in the body and transforms by manifesting the Way. It covers all time, all eras, all Buddhas, and all practices. If there were not practicing Buddha, there would be no casting off of attachment to Buddha and dharma. We would just be Buddha demons and dharma demons. Practice is the verification and the actualization of the enlightenment of all Buddhas—past, present, and future.

This is why practice and enlightenment are one. The minute you practice, you personally verify the realization of Shakyamuni Buddha. You personally verify the actualization of all the Buddhas throughout space and time. And that is enlightenment. Practice and enlightenment are one reality. If you want to transform ignorance into enlightenment, realize for yourself the power of the karma of invocation, vow, and practice. See how this karma functions in your own life.

The possibilities that compose the spectrum of human experience are your possibilities. All space and all time come alive in each one of us. How we practice and realize our lives depends on what we invoke, what we call forth. Regardless of whether we appreciate this fact or not, we are ceaselessly invoking. So, what will it be? Will it be greed, or will it be compassion? Will it be anger, or will it be wisdom? Will it be ignorance, or will it be enlightenment? It is all in our hands. How do we invoke vow, and practice that vow in our lives? We should examine this question thoroughly and keep examining it forever.

CHAPTER 4

Atonement:
Taking Responsibility

All evil karma ever committed by me since of old,
Because of my beginningless greed, anger, and ignorance,
Born of my body, mouth, and thought,
Now I atone for it all.

Many rites of passage that take place in the context of Buddhist practice include the Gatha of Atonement near the beginning of the ceremony. The Gatha of Atonement, or At-one-ment, creates a pure and unconditioned state of consciousness. It initiates an attitude of mind conducive to entering the rite of passage, a mind receptive and open to transformation. Rites of passage mark the entrance point into different realms, relationships, or states of being.

Taking the precepts as one's life is a serious matter.

When we vow to maintain them, making a commitment to manifest our life with the wisdom and compassion of the Tathagata, we indeed enter a different realm. And in that passage, the Gatha of Atonement establishes a clean slate.

Before a student actually arrives at this point, much hard work has already been accomplished. The practice of Zen, as well as the practice of the precepts, begins with a sense of inquiry. Before we enter, we search. If there is no search, the cup is full. There is no place to put the tea. When Master Te-shan, an academic expert in the Diamond Sutra, came to southern China, he was on a mission. He came to show the barbarians in the south that "the special transmission outside the scriptures" was utter nonsense.

He was indignant, full of himself, not able even to consider that there was anything to seek. There was no opportunity for Te-shan to learn anything. He had all the answers. He knew; he was very clear on that. The great doubt was not raised until his encounter with an old woman selling cakes by the roadside. She offered him one of her cakes for free if he could answer a question. Quoting a line from the Diamond Sutra, she asked, "If past mind, future mind, and present mind are ungraspable, with which mind will the venerable monk eat this cake?" Te-shan was unable to answer.

At this point the question appeared for him and his search began. The cup was turned upside down. The spiritual search begins when we open our mind and heart, raising to consciousness the possibility inherent in human life. We call it raising the bodhi mind. This raising of the bodhi mind simply means seeing, hearing, feeling, experiencing, and realizing in ways that were not even imagined before. It means opening the doors of perception and awareness.

My own experience with Buddhist liturgy stands in my mind as a good example of this shift in the level of perceiving and appreciating. As a monk I participated in hundreds of services and ceremonies. I sat through them, chanted and bowed my way through them, and I did not get it. I couldn't hear it. It didn't touch me. Then one day it all turned inside out. The invisible became visible. I have no idea how it happened. Not only did I start to see, hear, feel, and realize what the meaning of liturgy was, but it also assaulted my whole body and mind. It opened my eyes—not gently but by ripping my eyelids off. It pierced my heart like nothing had ever pierced it before. Why did that shift occur? I understood the chants before. I appreciated their meaning. I was clear on what was taking place. I knew the logic of the rituals. Yet, somehow, it did not touch me. Why? It is one of those mysteries. Why do people fall in love? Sometimes it happens with somebody that you have known for a long time. Suddenly there is "love." A whole transformation takes place.

Usually, out of that transformation and opening emerges practice. And practice is doing. Practice means commitment and action. We are no longer observers standing on the sidelines. We become participants. Unfortunately, simply to participate in the ceremony does not guarantee any results. I have given the precepts to probably 150 people in the fifteen years we have been at Zen Mountain Monastery. There are a number of recipients who disappeared from training within months of going through the ceremony. Some people think that receiving the precepts is like getting a badge of some sort, their diploma assuring them a better moral life. They consider themselves graduated after jukai. I advise some people who are persistent about receiving the precepts to wait. I ask them to let their practice mature. I do that when I have a feeling that the request to receive the precepts is not happening for the right reasons. It may be more a matter of hierarchy or status within the community than a matter of the heart.

The transformation associated with the rite of passage does not take place just because you go through the ritual. There needs to be the search that brings you to the point of inquiry, and there needs to be a raising of the bodhi mind. That raising of consciousness needs to have taken place; otherwise, a new way of seeing, hearing, feeling, and realizing doesn't happen.

With practice—the doing, the commitment, the action—there comes discovery and realization. As a result, the precepts begin to be actualized as our own life. We make conscious, in a very personal way, the identity of the life-stream of the Buddhas and ancestors with the life-stream of all sentient beings. Not the life-stream of the Buddhas and ancestors in identity with our life-stream alone, but the life-stream of the Buddhas and ancestors in identity with all sentient beings, which, of course, includes oneself.

Real atonement takes place only when the bodhi mind has been raised and practice is engaged. When that has happened, we're dealing with a very powerful spiritual magnet that attracts everything into the sphere of practice. Raising the bodhi mind, practice and enlightenment thus become one reality.

All evil karma ever committed by me since of old. Every cause has an effect, and every effect is the next cause. But we should always appreciate the fact that cause and effect are one; they are not two distinct events. Cause does not precede effect, and effect does not follow cause. This is why karma does not move in only one direction. Remarkably, it moves backward in time and space as well as forward in time and space. It permeates the ten directions.

Because of my beginningless greed, anger, and ignorance. Greed, anger, and ignorance are the three poisons. They are the basis of evil karma. Transformed, they become the three virtues—compassion, wisdom, and enlightenment—and these qualities are the basis of good karma. They describe a way of being in harmony with the nature of all things.

Born of my body, mouth, and thought. Body, mouth, and thought are the spheres of action where karma is created, both good and evil. What we do with our bodies, what we do with our words, and what we do with our thoughts, all lead to consequences, all establish specific karma. We should appreciate this fact thoroughly.

Body language speaks outwardly and inwardly. When you clench your fists and grit your teeth, you create anger mentally and physically. When you place your hands in the cosmic mudra, you create a state of consciousness that reflects introspection and peace. What we do with our bodies is who we are. It is for that reason that the posture of zazen is so important.

When we bow, we manifest the body karma of the three virtues. When we gassho, we manifest the body karma of the three virtues. It is nearly impossible to communicate the meaning of this in words. Most of it is a process of personal discovery. If you just sit cross-legged and make the cosmic mudra with your hands, you may appreciate how that mudra affects your whole being, how it can turn your attention inward to the deepest aspects of yourself. There are other mudras, some that turn you outward, toward the world, but all of them are about the karma of body.

Words are also karma. What we say has a tremendous impact on our lives and on the world around us. When we vow to attain the Way, we connect with the karma of that vow. In chanting the name of the Buddha, we are one with the Buddha. There is no separation. On the other hand, "God, give me a Mercedes" creates an immediate separation. When our words are motivated by compassion and wisdom, they manifest as wisdom and compassion. When our words are motivated by greed, anger, and ignorance, that's what they manifest. When we express goodwill, we create the karma of goodwill. When we express anger, we create the karma of anger.

There is also the illusive karma of thought, which is all too often unrecognized. Thought, in and of itself, has the ability to transform. Actually, transformation can occur in all three spheres, but generally we pay little attention to the cause-and-effect power of thought. We think it is a very personal, invisible process and that nobody knows about it. But thoughts radiate like signals from a telecommunication satellite. We project what we are thinking in hundreds of ways. What we think touches the world and it touches us.

When thoughts move inward, and these thoughts are thoughts of greed, anger, and ignorance, we end up chewing up our own bodies. We end up destroying ourselves. This happens on both an individual and a collective level. Sometimes it is easy to see this in people's faces: somebody who is fifty years old looks a hundred; somebody who is a hundred years old looks fifty. Why? It is about body, mouth, and thought. It is karma that creates who we are, how we live our lives, how we relate to one another, and how we relate to ourselves. It is that simple and that important.

Now I atone for it all. When at-one-ment takes place with the whole body and mind, you have created a state that is pure and unconditioned. Spiritual realization and moral action are one reality. They are codependent—just like cause and effect. Enlightenment is not beyond good and evil, as popularized and consumerized Zen would have us believe. It is rather a way of using one's body and mind and living one's life with a clear and unequivocal moral commitment. Enlightenment is realized and actualized not only in the realm of good and evil but also within all dualities, and is at the same time not stained by those dualities. To take the Gatha of Atonement is to enter the practice of the precepts with the whole body and mind, prepared to make the enlightenment of all Buddhas, past and present, one's true self.

CHAPTER 5

Taking Refuge in the Three Treasures:
Waking Up

When I listen to the precepts, the vows, and the service dedications, when I feel my body in the bows, when I connect with the Buddhas and ancestors in the daily liturgy, I am touched by an incredible sense of gratitude for having the opportunity to hear, experience, and participate in these teachings at this time. I know it is a gift that I will never be able to repay. It makes me wonder how often any of us appreciates how profound this practice is. Do we really hear it? Do we sense it? Do we feel it with our bones, right down to the marrow, with every cell in our bodies— or is it just another fling, a dharma fling? It is vitally important to appreciate this life. In one sense, that is what taking refuge in the Three Treasures really is about, appreciating our life, appreciating all life, waking up again and again to that feeling.

People ask, "How can I deepen the teacher-student relationship?" It is like asking, "How can I love you?" Is there a book of instructions on how to love? Does the baby get taught how to love its mother, the flowers, the earth, and the rain? In Zen training we say, "Really put yourself into it," but what does that mean? It means to take refuge and to be protected by the Three Treasures. What are the Three Treasures? We chant, "Being one with the Buddha, being one with the Dharma, being one with the Sangha." Those are the Three Treasures, but what does it mean to "be one with"? This is what we need to see, to realize clearly and personally.

The way we use the word *refuge* is taken from the Japanese term *kie-ei*. *Kie-ei* consists of two characters. *Kie* means "to unreservedly throw oneself into," no holding back, no way out, no safety net, harness, or rope. That is the way you work with a koan—unreservedly. That is the way a parent rescues a child who is in danger. The parent does not think about himself or herself. The parent does not hesitate for a second. The second character, *ei,* literally means "to rely upon," in the way that a child leaps into a parent's arms, trusting unequivocally.

I remember when my children were young. They were able to stand by themselves but couldn't yet walk, and I would stand them up on the dresser and say, "Jump!" They would throw themselves into space, knowing I would be there. They had a complete sense of trust and unwavering commitment. It was total doing. "Unreservedly throwing oneself into and relying upon" differs from "a shelter or protection from danger or distress"—the more common definition of the word *refuge.*

Before we can appreciate *kie-ei,* we need to appreciate what it is we are relying upon and unreservedly throwing ourselves into—the Buddha, the Dharma, and the Sangha. Usually, we understand Buddha to be the historical Buddha. From an inclusive perspective, we say that all beings are Buddha. Also, Buddha is the teacher. We see Dharma as being the teachings of the Buddha, the medicine to heal the sickness, and sometimes it is the ten thousand things. We understand Sangha as the practitioners of the Buddha's Dharma, our companions along the way, and we also understand it as the whole phenomenal universe, all sentient beings.

Then, there is a much deeper way to appreciate these Three Treasures. Perhaps if we appreciate them deeply enough, we will realize what it means to take refuge in the Buddha, the Dharma, and the Sangha; to vow to save all sentient beings, to put an end to desires, to master the dharmas, and to accomplish the Way. Perhaps we will understand what it means to be one with this unwavering lineage of ancestors who have handed down this dharma from generation to generation, without holding anything back. They gave their lives to it: not three months, six months, a year, five or ten years, but their whole lives. They turned themselves inside out. They renounced everything else to make the Way clear. Why? So we can have it, here and now, served to us on a platter. It is ours for the taking. All we have to do is reach out.

What does it mean to reach out? It means to have exhaustively asked the questions: What is Buddha? What is Dharma? What is Sangha? What does it mean to take refuge? What does it mean to vow? What does it mean to be one with? What does it mean to commit? What does it mean to have a relationship with a teacher? The answers are all available. Nothing is hidden.

We can find it in books. We can find it in the sutras.

We can find it by asking. And, most important, we can find it simply by looking into ourselves. Why do we practice? What is it that we seek? What is it that we want? What is it that we are prepared to do to get what we want? Are we willing to practice the edge, take a risk, unreservedly throw ourselves into practice? Or are we just being opportunistic and calculating, ready only to skim a little cream off the top to take care of the immediate problems, but not ready to go to the depths?

The Three Treasures can be seen in many different ways. One way of understanding them is as the unified Three Treasures. The Buddha Treasure, from the perspective of the unified Three Treasures, is *anuttara-samyak-sambodhi,* perfect enlightenment. No one is without it. It does not increase one bit in Buddhas, nor is it reduced one bit in "ordinary" beings. It is our fundamental nature, the fundamental nature of each and every one of us. It is the essential reality of this great earth and of the universe. It is vast. It is empty. It is without self-nature. The virtues of the dharma of wisdom and liberation emerge from *anuttara-samyaksambodhi.* It is from here that we realize the three bodies of the Buddha— Dharmakaya, Sambhogakaya, and Nirmanakaya.

From the perspective of the unified Three Treasures, the Dharma Treasure is undefiled purity. There is neither a speck of defilement nor a single particle of ego in the Dharma Treasure. The Dharma reaches everywhere. There is nothing outside it. Where could the defilement possibly come from? Dharma embraces everything. It is for that reason it is pure and undefiled.

From the perspective of the unified Three Treasures, the Sangha Treasure is virtue and merit of harmony. What we call harmony is really the fusion of the Buddha

Treasure and the Dharma Treasure. Buddha, or fundamental nature, is empty of all characteristics, yet there is
an arising of karma, cause and effect, which is dharma
nature. There is this arising of causation, or dharma, yet
fundamental nature is empty. This vital matter is the life
of each one of us.

Another way of looking at the Three Treasures is as
the manifested Three Treasures. Direct realization of
bodhi is called the Buddha Treasure. Buddha was the first
person to realize bodhi. Each generation thereafter has
rekindled that realization as personal experience.
Enlightened masters opened their eyes and transmitted it
from generation to generation, from country to country.
That is the manifested Buddha Treasure.

The Dharma of the manifested Three Treasures is
the Buddha's realization. That realization of the Buddha
is at once the realization of all sentient beings, past, present, and future; your life and my life.

The Sangha of the manifested Three Treasures is the
practicing of the Buddha's dharma. The moment two people get together and practice—not just go through the gestures, take the form, use the vernacular, or dress in the
clothing—but practice with the heart, mind, and body;
with commitment, vow, and dedication; with great faith,
great doubt, and great determination—then you have the
manifested Sangha Treasure. Everything else is a cheap
imitation. It just looks like the real thing.

Finally we come to the abiding Three Treasures.
"Converting *devas* and liberating people, appearing in
vast space or in a speck of dust, is the Buddha Treasure of
the abiding Three Treasures." To abide means to preserve
and protect. We need to appreciate that our practice is
not only about our own realization, about relieving our

own pain and suffering; it is also about relieving the pain and suffering of all beings. We should never lose sight of that. We remind ourselves every night of that fact at the monastery by reciting the bodhisattva vows.

We are the vessel of the dharma at this time and this place. What we do each sitting, each moment, with our work, with our zazen and services, with our vows, not only affirms and verifies the enlightenment of the Buddha and all the past Buddhas but also preserves and protects the dharma so it will be available for future generations.

We are part of the transmission of the dharma from East to West. It goes from place to place only through people. Only a Buddha can realize Buddha. Only a Buddha can practice Buddha-dharma. Only a Buddha is a vessel of the dharma. All sentient beings are Buddhas. All Buddhas are sentient beings. What we do, therefore, is no small thing. Our actions have far-reaching consequences. The karma of taking refuge, of making the vow to save all sentient beings, vowing to realize oneself, to practice zazen, to nurture the mountains and rivers, to work in the garden—all of it is part of the legacy that has come down to us for twenty-five hundred years and, it is hoped, will continue twenty-five hundred years into the future. If it does, it is because of how we take care of it.

We include in the abiding Buddha Treasure those Buddhas made of wood, metal, stone, and paint. All of them are manifestations of the infinite boundless Buddhas present in the myriad realms. Each of these Buddhas is presently expounding the dharma, converting and saving all beings, healing and nourishing all beings, according to the karma of circumstances. Do we really understand the truth of that statement? The wooden Buddha on the altar is expounding the dharma according to karma; how do we understand that? Common sense is not going to help us here. Scientific knowledge is not going to help us. There is another realm of human experience involved.

What does it mean to bow to the Buddha, specifically to that wooden Buddha on the altar? A monk asked Chao-chou, "What is Buddha?" Chao-chou said, "He's on the altar." What did Chao-chou mean? How is that piece of wood a Buddha? Is that painting a Buddha? Do not separate yourself from anything! Do not separate yourself from Mu. Do not separate yourself from the chanting, from your vow, from your commitment, from each other, from this whole great earth.

"Transformed into the sutras and converted into the oceanic storehouse, the Dharma of the abiding Three Treasures delivers the inanimate and animate, saving all beings." What are the sutras? The spirit of these precepts, the spirit of the sutras, the spirit of this discourse, goes far beyond the words. We cannot reach them with our analytical minds alone. This teaching is dark to the mind; we have to sense it with our heart, our feelings.

The Sangha of the abiding Three Treasures is saving all beings from all suffering, releasing them from the abode of the three realms—the realms of desire, form, and formlessness. In order to save all beings from suffering, we need to put an end to the three poisons of greed, anger, and ignorance.

Having appreciated the Three Treasures from the three different perspectives, we need to appreciate the unity or the oneness of these three perspectives. Each interpenetrates the other. The Buddha, the Dharma, and the Sangha completely merge and are one reality. What is that reality? This dharma is incredibly profound and infinitely subtle. Because of its profundity and subtlety, it requires whole body and mind engagement for it to communicate.

Taking refuge is not a matter of casual encounter. This is a whole body-and-mind vow, whole body-and-mind unity, whole body-and-mind commitment. Those who give that much, realize it. Those who do not, do not realize it. Some may realize it, some may not. Either way is okay. It is up to us. Nobody can do it for us. Buddha could not do it for us, if he were here. Only we have the power to take advantage of the personal karma that has placed us in this time and place. It is a unique opportunity, and how we use it is totally in our hands.

In order to reach our full human potential, we must live completely and die completely. In order for this practice to function, it needs to be engaged. It does not happen automatically because we wrap a rakusu around our neck, put on a robe, attend a retreat, or read a book on Zen—"Okay, I'm here. Now do me, Dharma." It does not happen that way. We have to work for it. We have to put ourselves on the line. We have to practice the edge of our life in order to receive the dharma. Undeniably, it is here. We are surrounded, interpenetrated, enveloped, and swallowed by it. But most of us are blind and deaf to it. We do not see it. We do not hear it. We do not feel it. When will we wake up?

CHAPTER 6

The First Pure Precept:
Not Creating Evil

In most of the traditional koan collections, there are no cases that deal directly with the precepts. The classical koans tend to focus on self-realization, within which moral and ethical realization is implicit, but usually the moral and ethical teachings are not addressed explicitly. This is one of the reasons why the precepts are a neglected area of practice. To counter that tendency, I have introduced several koans on the precepts in the collection of cases coming out of Zen Mountain Monastery, among them the three koans on the Pure Precepts included in this book. On the surface, the Three Pure Precepts—Not creating evil, Practicing good, and Actualizing good for others—seem rather simplistic. In reality, they are a bottomless source of teachings, critically relevant in our day-to-day practice of Zen. We should be sure to study them carefully.

The prologue to this koan regarding the first pure precept introduces the dilemma of dualistic thinking:

The moment there is the slightest choice of good and evil, your mind falls into confusion. If you are not caught up in the rules and ranks, there is no seeking. Then tell me, what particular course of moral action is to be taken? At this point, if there is any trace of concept or contrivance, you are a demon haunting the fields and forests. Do you understand? If not, listen to the following. If you do understand, listen to the following. The moment there is the slightest choice of good and evil, your mind falls into confusion.

The first line in the prologue is a reference to "picking and choosing," the phrase that appears in the opening lines of the "Faith Mind Sutra" by the third ancestor, Seng-ts'an. In making a choice, there is always a separation. In intimacy, that separation dissolves. How does that intimacy unfold and manifest through the precepts?

On several occasions the great Chinese Zen master Chao-chou used the "Faith Mind Sutra" as the starting point of his teachings with students:

Once, a monastic asked Chao-chou, "How can you avoid picking and choosing?" Chao-chou answered, "Between heaven and earth, I alone am the honored one." The monastic continued, "That's picking and choosing." Chao-chou responded, "Asshole! Where's the picking and choosing?"

The intimacy that encompasses heaven and earth is where the precepts begin. We constantly need to be reminded not to attach to anything. It is very easy to understand not attaching to things that are evil—not attaching to things that are dualistic. But the same problem exists if we attach to Buddhism, or to the absolute. Half of the koans dealt with in traditional Zen training are about monastics stuck "on top of the mountain," unable to manifest their realization in the ten thousand things, unable to descend back into the world of choices, demands, and confusion.

Picking and choosing can refer to the precepts or anything we can attach ourselves to. Attachment needs two things: the thing attached to and the person attaching. No matter how wonderful or valuable the precepts are, when you attach to them, they become a set of rules that come in from the outside rather than being a manifestation of one's life. When that happens, they become a hindrance. That is when they bind a person rather than help one to realize the inherent freedom of all beings. No matter how valuable and wonderful gold dust is, when it gets in our eyes, it blinds us. Anything we attach to has that potential to blind us to what is real.

If you are not caught up in the rules and ranks, there is no seeking. The "rules and ranks" can refer to the precepts. Can you see how Chao-chou is utterly free? He's asking, How do you avoid being caught up in the precepts while still practicing and functioning vibrantly with them? In allowing them to become guidelines in your life, how will you prevent them from becoming a cage? In dismissing them, how will you know what particular course of moral action to take?

At this point, if there is any trace of concept or contrivance, you are a demon haunting the fields and forests. If our understanding of the teachings is mere absorption of information that has come from the outside, then it has not yet become embodied and touched our bones. Real understanding arrives only from our own experience. The imperative remains: Do not look for rules and patterns; realize the teachings as your own life.

Do you understand? If not, listen to the following.

Not understanding means it has not yet been communicated. Not understanding may also indicate blank consciousness. Understanding can mean clinging to the words and ideas. Neither of these positions reaches the truth. These precepts are about *prajna* wisdom. They are not about information or knowledge. It is not about the words and ideas that describe reality. It is the direct pointing and realization of the reality itself. How do we go beyond understanding and not understanding? *Listen to the following.*

The main case of the koan presents a question and a response about the nature of evil. *"Not creating evil" is the true teaching of all Buddhas. How do you not create evil? We must first understand the relationship between evil and its creation. It is not just the donkey looking at the well but also the donkey looking at the donkey, the well looking at the well, beings looking at beings, mountains looking at mountains. Because of this truth, there is "not creating evil."*

"Not creating evil" is the fundamental teaching of Buddhism. It is the central pillar of our practice. The line "It is not just the donkey looking at the well but also the donkey looking at the donkey, the well looking at the well" comes from Great Master Dogen's *Three Hundred Koan Shobogenzo.* Ts'ao-shan asked the head monastic, "The true Dharmakaya of all the Buddhas is like an empty sky. It corresponds to the form of itself like the moon reflected in the water. How do you explain the way it manifests?" The pure Dharmakaya is the absolute basis of reality. Ts'ao-shan is essentially asking the monastic to explain how the absolute basis of reality manifests in the world. The head monastic responded, "It's like a donkey looking at a well." Ts'ao-shan said, "Saying it that way is true, but still you've only said eighty or ninety percent of it." The

head monastic then asked, "How about you, Master?"
Ts'ao-shan said, "It's like the well looking at the donkey."

Dogen picked this up and used it as a teaching in his
fascicle "The Thirty-seven Conditions Favorable to
Enlightenment." In it he said, "When a donkey looks into
a well, donkey sees donkey, well sees well. They are unified and inseparable." He is speaking of the interpenetration of all things, the codependency and mutual causality
that permeates the Diamond Net of Indra.

In another fascicle he took this up in the form in
which we use it in this koan. *"Not creating evil," he says,
is not just the donkey looking at the well but also the well
looking at the well, the donkey looking at the donkey,
human beings looking at human beings, mountains looking at mountains. Because such a principle exists, that is,
the relationship between evil and its creation, we must
refrain from evil. Buddha's true dharma body is like
space, like vast space, or like the moon reflected in the
water. Since all things are refraining from evil, all forms
are not creating evil. It is like space existing no matter
where you point, it is like the moon reflected in the water.
This kind of "not creating evil" is surely actualized.*

In Section XVI of the Diamond Sutra, entitled
"Purgation through Suffering the Retribution for Past
Sins," there is the following passage:

*Furthermore, Subhuti, if it be that good men and
good women, who receive and retain this discourse, are
downtrodden, their evil destiny is the inevitable retribu-
tive result of sins committed in their past lives. By virtue
of their present misfortunes, the reacting effects of their
pasts will be thereby worked out, and they will be in a
position to attain the consummation of incomparable
enlightenment.*

If beings are anguished, oppressed, in pain, this is

the result of past karma. The causes or actions that have created the effects that they are now experiencing are in their past. In the process of experiencing their current suffering, they are working out that karma, being at one with it.

The causes of evil karma are greed, anger, and ignorance—the three poisons. We create karma through action, by what we do with our body, words, and thoughts. In atoning, we take full and unequivocal responsibility for it all. When we do that, we empower ourselves. It becomes *our* evil karma, not someone else's. We acknowledge ourselves as active agents, not passive victims. We begin to recognize that our life is not just something that happens to us.

Further on in this discourse, the Buddha says, "You should know, Subhuti, that the significance of this discourse is beyond conception; likewise, the fruit of its rewards is beyond conception." This is not a matter of accumulated knowledge. "The extent and value of its meaning and importance cannot be materially gauged. The meaning must be realized because it cannot be understood without direct experience." To attain their true meaning, these words have to be realized.

"By virtue of their present misfortunes, the reacting effects of their pasts will be thereby worked out, and they will be in a position to attain the consummation of incomparable enlightenment." In one way or another, this is what I constantly say to students who feel unable to be the koan Mu, the sound of one hand, or the original face. Anything that we cling to separates us from the koan. It distances us from our life. There cannot be falling away of body and mind when the mind is moving. When the mind moves and there is a witness, there is a constant reaffirmation of the illusion that there is a self. When there is a thinker, subject and object are polarized. Mu is over here and we are over there. The only way to see Mu is to be Mu—one thing, one reality. That means forgetting the self. And you cannot forget the self if you are constantly re-creating it.

That continuous creation of the self is karma. It is the substance of the past that has not been dealt with and let go of. Our "present misfortunes" have to be worked out. It doesn't work to suppress them. If a thought constantly recurs, we need to let it run its course, exhaust, and complete itself. Only then can we unify its cause and effect.

We should reflect a moment on the structure of the precepts ceremony and how it relates to this particular precept. In offering the Gatha of Atonement, we establish an atmosphere of receptiveness and purity. What does purity mean? How is a being or an action unadulterated and without defilement? We say that "all dharmas are purity." Purity reaches everywhere. It fills the whole universe; in fact, it is the universe itself. This is what at-one-ment means: being one. There must be constant atonement in order for us to return to the precepts. Practice does not stop after enlightenment; it continues endlessly.

After the Gatha of Atonement, we take refuge in the Three Treasures. The Three Treasures, the Three Pure Precepts, and the Ten Grave Precepts together form the Sixteen Precepts of the Buddha Way. Taking refuge in the Three Treasures means being one with the Three Treasures—being one with the Buddha, being one with the Dharma, being one with the Sangha. It means unification and mutual identity. The Three Pure Precepts essentially define the order of harmony in the universe. In the harmonious universe there is "not creating evil," there is the "practice of good," and there is the "actualization of good for others." The Ten Grave Precepts are the functioning of the Three Pure Precepts. In other words, they answer the question, How? How do you "not create evil," how do you "practice good," and how do you "actualize good for others?"

The Three Pure Precepts are pure because they are absolute. They are pure because they reach everywhere. Evil has no independent existence. It is dependent upon its creator. The same can be said for the entire phenomenal universe, and for each one of us. We are all codependent entities.

When you look at the Ten Grave Precepts from the perspective of the Three Pure Precepts, "not creating evil" is Do not kill, do not steal, do not misuse sexuality, do not lie, do not cloud the mind, do not speak of others' errors and faults, do not elevate the self and blame others, do not be withholding, do not be angry, and do not defile the Three Treasures. "Practicing good" is the other side of "not creating evil." "Practicing good" is Affirm life, be giving, honor the body, manifest truth, proceed clearly, see the perfection, realize self and other as one, give generously, actualize harmony, and experience the intimacy of things.

Each of the Ten Grave Precepts expresses how not to create evil and how to practice good. One side is affirmative; one side is prohibitive. They work together. They are interdependent and arise mutually. "Actualizing good for others" is nothing other than the mutual identity of "not creating evil" and "practicing good." It is the great heart of Kannon Bodhisattva manifesting in the world as compassion.

Good and evil are very difficult to define because moral values are relative. They are relative to culture, species, personal preference, and social customs; to time, place, position, and degree. Because it is difficult to nail this down, we return to the fundamental understanding of the Three Pure Precepts. Good is understood differently in different worlds and different times. Still, the human mind is originally neither good nor evil. Good and evil always arise in accord with circumstances. They are created. "Not creating" is therefore quintessential.

The unique contribution of the Buddhist precepts in the domain of religious morality is that they go beyond moral excellence. What they address is how to protect morality from legalism, conformity, and moralism. While maintaining authenticity and freedom, we do not retreat from moral involvement. It is because people do not fully understand what is meant by "the human mind is originally beyond good and evil" that we entertain the deluded view that Zen is somehow amoral. Unequivocally, Zen is not beyond morality. Zen functions in the world of good and evil. At the same time, it is not hindered by good and evil. That is the moral freedom of these incredible teachings.

Essentially, the nature of morality is empty. To realize that does not, however, lead to nihilism or anarchy. Realization does not entail an "anything goes" attitude. The pivotal focus of practice with the precepts is how to live in the world of relativity without falling into the trap of being distracted and disturbed by the ten thousand things. How do we realize absolute freedom and purity in the midst of a world fragmented by good and evil?

Since good and evil have no metaphysical ground or independent self-nature, how do they spring into being? How does evil appear? By creating. That is why not creating any evil is intrinsic to realization, intrinsic to enlightenment. In other words, to commit evil is incompatible with enlightenment. Enlightenment without morality is not authentic enlightenment. From a Buddhist point of view, morality can never be fully authenticated without enlightenment. Morality and enlightenment are thoroughly interdependent.

Enlightened or deluded, we all live within the intricate maze of the laws of cause and effect. It is an inescapable fact that morality functions in the world of duality. The precepts exist to deal with that infinite range of phenomena. They are based on absolute nature and emerge out of the realization of no-self. But no-self does not function. The functioning of the wisdom of absolute nature manifests as the precepts, as compassion.

Evil is neither nonexistent nor existent; there is simply "not creating." Evil is neither empty nor formed; there is simply "not creating." Evil is not moral, amoral, or moralistic but simply "not creating." In Buddhism, there is no "thou shall not" coming down to us from on high. "I will not," reflecting a kind of self-centered autonomy, does not apply, either. What the precepts are about is noncontrivance—not a thought moves. Morality, if it is going to be authentic, can and must arise spontaneously from enlightenment. Morality and enlightenment are not to be understood in terms of cause and effect, or means and end.

When morality becomes effortless, purposeless, and playful, it becomes the nonmoral morality of the Buddhas and ancestors. That is the culmination of formal Zen training. At that time, morality, art, and play merge together as one thing. One teacher said, "When 'ought' becomes 'is' in the transparency of thusness, only then do we come to the highest morality."

How do you not create evil? We must first understand the relationship between evil and its creation. It is not just "the donkey looking at the well but also the donkey looking at the donkey, the well looking at the well, beings looking at beings, mountains looking at mountains. Because of this truth, there is not creating evil." This is a statement of mutual arising and identity. Every aspect and juncture contains the totality. That is the way it is with thought and reality. That is the way it is with the senses—the eye, the form that the eye sees, and consciousness together create what we call reality. They are interdependent—one cannot exist without the other.

The verse in this koan is an expression of that interdependence:

> The whole universe and its myriad forms,
> Heavens and hells,
> Are all used without hindrance;
> Compounding medicines to heal the sickness,
> Creating sickness to heal the medicine.

The ten thousand things do not obstruct one another. Interpenetration and interdependence exist mutually, without hindrance. They do not get in each other's way. Water does not hinder water. "The whole universe and its myriad forms," the ten thousand things, "are all used without hindrance"—action. In a sense, the precepts are a medicine compounded to heal the sickness of evil karma. They eradicate greed, anger, and ignorance. When, through realization, you turn the three poisons around, greed becomes compassion, anger becomes wisdom, and ignorance becomes enlightenment. The pairs are interwoven parts of the same reality. "Compounding medicines to heal the sickness" is the functioning of the precepts. All the teachings—zazen, liturgy, work practice, face-to-face teaching—are medicines compounded to heal the sickness.

"Creating sickness to heal the medicine." There are

all kinds of sicknesses that need to be created for different kinds of medicines. Sometimes there is a sickness that needs to be created when the use of a medicine has been completed but we are still attached to it. A new sickness can cut through that attachment and heal. Sometimes we have to heal the sickness of having no sickness. That is the most difficult ailment to heal.

When we hold on to the precepts, we are trapped in the cage of the precepts, not heeding the warning in the prologue: "The moment there is the slightest choice of good and evil, your mind falls into confusion." If you get caught up in the hierarchies or the grid of rules, if there is any trace of concept or contrivance, you are like a demon haunting the fields, trapped in a self-created labyrinth. With the slightest choice of good and evil, your mind falls into confusion. If those precepts are used as rules, they lose a lot of their value. We get stuck in them. When Kannon Bodhisattva with her ten thousand hands is responding to the cries of the world, there is no contrivance, no concept, no knowing. She has no idea of what she is doing—she is blind, deaf, and dumb. That in itself is not creating evil.

If we are not aware of the precepts, of their existence, of how Buddhas live their life in the world of samsara, then it is very easy to go on our way, merrily creating all sorts of karma. But once we are aware of the precepts and see that there does exist a way of understanding how we fit into this vast universe, how we can function in a way that is nourishing and healing and in harmony with things, we create a cutting edge to work with. That cutting edge is a challenge to each one of us. It is one thing to cast off body and mind, it is quite another thing to have realized "cast-off body and mind" and to manifest that realization in the world. At that point, our way of perceiving ourselves and the universe, of combusting our lives among the ten thousand things, is completely transformed.

CHAPTER 7

The Second Pure Precept:
Practicing Good

M aster Dogen said: *Practice all that is good. All that is good is the good of the three natures—good, bad, and neutral. Although good exists within the nature of good, it does not mean that good has some previous, independent existence and is waiting to be accomplished. When good is done, it contains all good. Although good is formless, when it is done, it attracts more good faster than a magnet attracts iron. Its power is stronger than the strongest wind. All the accumulated karma throughout the earth, mountains, rivers, world, and lands cannot obstruct the power of good.*

The Three Pure Precepts are an open-ended and very profound teaching. In the world, they manifest as the Ten Grave Precepts. When the ground out of which the Three Pure Precepts emerge hasn't been fully appreciated, there is always the danger that the Ten Grave Precepts will degenerate into a mere collection of rules. That is not what the precepts are. The precepts are a way of life that has to be intimately experienced, digested, and actualized. As we work with the second pure precept, "Practice good," we should keep in mind the power of what we're dealing with and attend to it with great care.

We say that the precepts are the definition of the life of a Buddha; they describe how an enlightened being lives in the world. Early in their practice students have not had that premise confirmed by their experience. They have the word of the teacher, the ancestors, and the sutras to go by, but they do not know it personally. And it is personal experience that is the bottom line in this practice, not understanding or belief. Zen is a practice that requires one to empower oneself, to realize for oneself everything that the Buddhas and ancestors have realized for themselves. That in itself is the mind-to-mind transmission.

As practice evolves, the precepts, originally accepted as an act of faith, become the very fabric of our life. This transformation occurs if the practice is conducted properly. By the time formal koan study is completed and the Five Ranks of Tung-shan that address the relationship of the relative and the absolute have been thoroughly mastered, a student is in a position to address the 120 koans on the precepts. The work with these koans is the verification that these precepts are no longer an external admonition but rather are a manifestation of one's life.

The practice of the precepts takes time. It continuously deepens and broadens. If the 120 precept koans were given to a student just beginning practice, there is no way the student would be able to see and realize them. Each step needs to evolve in an orderly way. The precepts are part of the transmission ceremony at the conclusion of formal training, handed down from generation to generation.

As such they are expected to be a part of the student's realization.

Recently, as I was watching my eighteen-year-old son washing his clothes, I thought about the evolution of how we learn to do our own laundry. It is generally known that ten-year-old kids do not want to wash their clothes—or anything else, for that matter. Their jeans can practically stand by themselves. There is no way parents can get their children to stay clean, pick up after themselves, close the doors, wipe their feet, or turn out the lights without relying on constant repetition and nagging.

Then, in late adolescence, something magical happens. Suddenly teenagers become aware of their sexuality. They start to brush their teeth and buy underarm deodorant sprays. The laundry, though, remains a tough problem. Kids still do not want to wash their clothes. They are just too involved with the many other important activities of their lives. But now there is the possibility of using *upaya*, skillful means, that was not available before.

Before he noticed the opposite sex, if I did not take his clothes and wash them, my son would wear them until they rotted on his body. Now the dirty clothes pile up in the laundry basket until they are five feet high. Everything he owns is in there. And I just wait for the insight to arrive. Suddenly one morning, as he is racing around getting ready for school, he realizes he has nothing to wear except something old and smelly. Obviously, all the girls will know that he is wearing the same shirt he wore the day before. He ends up putting it on and he is fuming, feeling betrayed, and that night he washes his clothes. This process repeats itself: within two or three weeks, as the clothes are exhausted, the same phenomenon happens. After three or four years, a point is reached where the practice of doing one's laundry becomes automatic. It spontaneously arises out of one's very being.

It is the same with the practice of the precepts. In the beginning they are a collection of rules: do not kill, do not steal, do not elevate the self and put down others. Shut the door, turn out the light, wash the dishes. With time, we realize what the Three Pure Precepts really entail. We realize what the practice of the Ten Grave Precepts really means. We realize atonement. Then this matter of ongoing practice becomes very personal and immediate. Ultimately, the precepts interfuse with our life. People who have come to the "end" of their practice without the precepts as part of their lives probably do so because the precepts were never a part of their practice all along the way.

The opening statement of Dogen in this chapter is a koan. We take it up to explore the second pure precept. This koan begins with a prologue:

"Transcend all attachments, concepts, and views. Penetrate beyond all entanglements and dualities. And thus, the marvelous mind of nirvana is revealed. The true dharma eye is opened. The exquisite teaching of formless form is manifested. Actualized in the world of good and evil, it is not of good and evil. It is the endless spring of peaceful dwelling, reaching everywhere."

The three phrases—"marvelous mind of nirvana," "true dharma eye," and "exquisite teaching of formless form" were used by Shakyamuni Buddha when he transmitted the dharma to Mahakashyapa. The state of clarity described by these words is attained when we free ourselves of the entanglements of dualities, ridding ourselves of views, concepts, and attachments. It is not something acquired as a result of practice. It is something *revealed* as a result of practice. Once you come to realization, the teaching of formless form, the marvelous mind of nirvana, and the true dharma eye begin to actualize in the world of good and evil. This realization arises from a place where there is no good and no evil, no heaven and no earth; no eye, ear, nose, tongue, body, mind; no enlightenment, no delusion, no nirvana. Yet it manifests in a world where there is good and evil, heaven and hell, cause and effect. At the same time, it is not, in and of itself, good or evil.

"The endless spring" is a poetic way of referring to realization—the spring that never ends. When we accomplish ourselves, that peaceful dwelling is everywhere. It exists in the midst of evil and, at the same time, is unstained and untrammeled by it.

Good neither exists nor does not exist. It is simply practice. It is manifested through practice. "Practicing good" is practice itself. Good is not form; it is not emptiness: it is just practice. "Practicing good" falls into neither of those extremes. It is neither being nor nonbeing, neither existence nor nonexistence, neither form nor emptiness; it is just practice.

"Practicing good" is not a moral injunction but rather realization itself. It is not a contrivance. The moment the mind moves, it is no longer "practicing good." The witness that is always watching needs to dissolve, just like it does in zazen. If in your zazen, you are following the breath and you are watching yourself follow the breath, that scrutiny separates you from the breath. There can be no "falling away of body and mind." The witness, in noticing, is saying, "I exist." It constantly reaffirms the illusion that there is a self. The skin bag gets thicker and thicker.

Morality, in order to be authentic, needs to arise out of one's own realization. It is because the self is empty that "not creating evil," "practicing good," and "actualizing good for others" make any sense at all. When morality spontaneously springs forth from one's own attainment, it is effortless, purposeless, and even playful. It is a delightful morality.

The Sixteen Precepts of the Buddha Way are the most profound teaching of morality that I have ever seen. They are alive, vital, and responsive to circumstances. Good and evil are always conditioned and dependent upon circumstances. The whole phenomenal universe is nothing but conditioned existence. Every speck of dust is dependent upon everything else in the universe. You cannot affect one thing without affecting the totality.

We should understand, too, that good is not an object. It is not an entity or a condition that the practitioner deals with. It is just practicing. It does not exist independently but arises in accord with the circumstances, in the specific context of a particular time, place, position, and degree of action. A single event, seen from two different perspectives, can appear good from one angle and bad from another. Someone pointing a gun at me pulls the trigger: bad karma. He fires; I duck: good karma. The bullet hits the person standing behind me: bad karma. Same bullet, three scenarios. Good and evil always appear and operate within a reference system. They need to be seen in terms of that reference system in order for the action to be evaluated. So, time, place, position, and degree need to be considered in appreciating any action.

The historical period of time is tightly interwoven with the generally accepted notion of morality. There are scenes on television these days that were outrageous and censored twenty-five years ago. Language I used as a boatswain's mate in the navy in 1947, and was chewed out for by the officers, is common on prime-time programs today. What was inappropriate in the past is acceptable now.

Place also affects how an action appears. Wearing my priestly robes addressing an assembly of students is perfectly appropriate. Wearing my robes at the downtown diner is questionable. There is nothing wrong with the robes; it is the place that makes the difference. Customs that are perfectly acceptable in the United States may be taboo in Japan. Similarly, some conventions common in Japan are unacceptable here.

Soon after I arrived at the Zen Center of Los Angeles, somebody invited me to use a hot tub in the backyard surrounded by apartment buildings. After my first *sesshin*, I took my clothes off and jumped in. As I was sitting naked in the tub, in broad daylight, I mused, "Ah, California, it's so laid back and loose." At that point my teacher arrived and climbed into the hot tub with his bathing suit on. When it got too hot for me and I was getting out, he looked at me and said, "Daido! You don't have a bathing suit on!" Matter of factly, I said, "Well, I didn't think I needed one." "Of course you do!" he said. "I'm embarrassed. Look at all of the houses around us." I was somewhat startled because I knew that in Japan bathing naked communally is quite common and acceptable. Still, what my teacher was pointing out was that it was okay in Japan but not here, in this setting. Morality changed with the place.

The position or role we play in a relationship also makes all the difference in the world in how we function. What we do as a parent, what we do as a lover, and what we do as a teacher may differ dramatically. The act may be the same, but in those various roles the moral quality of the act shifts.

The degree of action, its intensity, is another parameter affecting the moral nature of an act. It needs to be just the right amount. It needs to match the encountered conditions. Sometimes a whisper is just as powerful and penetrating as a thunderous roar. Time, place, position, and degree form the matrix within which the precepts function.

Good and evil, self and other, absolute and relative, being and nonbeing, are all interrelated and interpenetrated entities. Good and evil occur in the world. Yet, even if evil envelops the entire earth and the whole universe, there is still "not creating evil" and "practicing good." "Not creating evil" and "practicing good" are not hindered at all by the omnipresence of evil. That is the depth and extent of the Pure Precepts and realization.

In speaking of our koan, Master Dogen said: *Since time immemorial, Buddhas and ancestors have continuously taught, "Practice good." Although good is practice and practice is good, it is not the self that does good, and it is not known to the self. Further, it is not other, nor is it known to the other. Practice is not being or nonbeing, not form or emptiness: it is just practice. In practice, all that is good is realized and actualized.*

In "practicing good" it is not the self that does good. The self is forgotten. "To forget the self is to be enlightened by the ten thousand things. To be enlightened by the ten thousand things is to cast away one's body and mind and the body and mind of others." That is the source of the Pure Precepts.

The presence of self, the subtlest hint of self-centeredness, creates the difference between a "do-gooder" and the manifestation of true compassion. In compassion, in practicing good, there is no agent that is doing good and no one who benefits from it; there is no subject or object. There is not even any sense of doing. Compassion happens. It happens the same way you grow your hair. There is no effort involved. It is not the self that does good; "the doing of good" is not even known to the self. Knowing depends on the words and ideas that describe reality. There is no intimacy in knowing. Knowing involves the knower and the thing that the knower knows, and that implies separation. This practice has nothing to do with knowledge. It is the experience of intimacy.

Doing good in complete intimacy is the embodiment and activity of the ten thousand hands and eyes of Kannon Bodhisattva. Kannon Bodhisattva, for those of you who have not met her, is the bodhisattva of compassion. She is called "the hearer of the cries of the world." She is the bodhisattva who responds when someone cries out for help. When she responds, she responds in perfect accord with circumstances. She doesn't always appear in the form of a goddess or even necessarily in a female form. She may appear in male form or in nonhuman form. She may appear as a god or devil. She responds without mind. There is no thought. Kannon does not know about goodness. She doesn't know about doing. Compassion arises spontaneously out of wisdom: the realization of no separation. Someone falls; you pick the person up. No effort.

I've mentioned Kannon Bodhisattva many times before. People wonder about such an esoteric teaching. Where is this goddess? Why don't we see her? Every time a car breaks down on the highway or a lonely road and a motorist stops to give aid, that's Kannon Bodhisattva manifesting in the form of a motorist coming to the aid of another. If she's going to help a drunk in a bar, she'll probably appear as another drunk, not as a holy being glowing with light.

It's kind of interesting how this happens. A couple of weeks ago I was watching a news report about two weimaraner dogs, 175 pounds each. The two of them broke loose and attacked a ten-year-old girl. The girl started screaming for help. Bursting out of a nearby house came this little woman. The broadcast had her on camera. She was kind of cut up and scarred and she couldn't have weighed more than a hundred pounds. She was short, almost like a bird. She had tied in to those dogs and started punching them, hitting them, pulling them, and throwing herself on top of the child. Finally she dragged the child into a swampy pond—it wasn't water, just a bunch of muck and mud. Somehow the muck and mud confused the dogs and broke them from their killer trance, and they ran off.

The reporter said to the woman, "You're a hero." And the woman seemed stunned by that. She was looking at the reporter quizzically. She said, "But the little girl cried out, 'Please help me! They're going to kill me.' Over and over again. How could I not go?" There was no sense of self in this woman's action. The girl wasn't her daughter. This woman was totally vulnerable, yet totally invulnerable because of no-self. This is the ten thousand hands and eyes of Kannon Bodhisattva. This is the intimacy of doing good with no attachment to self.

It's very easy to understand not attaching to things that are evil or dualistic. But the same problem exists when we attach to good, to Buddhism, to the absolute. Half of the koans we deal with are about monastics who are stuck on the top of the mountain, unable to manifest their realization amid the ten thousand things, unable to descend from the mountain back into the world. We need to realize that practice is not being or nonbeing, not form or emptiness: it is just practice. "Just practice" is suchness. It is this very moment, transcending all dualities.

"Just practice" contains no past and no future. It is always right here, right now.

The precepts are no small matter. To miss these basic moral teachings of the Buddha-dharma in our training is to miss the Buddha-dharma. We should make no mistake about that. Without morality, there is no enlightenment. Without enlightenment, there is no morality.

Here is the verse on this koan:

Empty and at ease, no hindrance,
Lofty and serene, reaching everywhere.
North of the South Pole, south of the North Pole—
Great peace.
Those who arrive here are rare indeed—
Right and wrong ended,
Standing alone on earth,
No trace remains.

It is because of emptiness that there is no hindrance. Reaching everywhere—this is the universe itself. Peace encompasses the whole of the great earth.

Someone asked me once during dokusan, "With so many teachers, monasteries, and practitioners, why are there so few people who realize themselves?" I really could not give a satisfactory answer. This is a difficult practice, no question about it. There are people who get their doctorates in four years, yet they practice for twelve years trying to see their first koan. That is not unusual.

Why should it be so difficult? In a way, it is; and in a way, it is not. In ancient China the Pang family took up this point during one of their famous dharma dialogues. Layman Pang, Laywoman Pang, and their daughter, all enlightened practitioners, were sitting around their living room. Layman Pang said, "Difficult, difficult, difficult—

like trying to find a needle in the haystack." Laywoman Pang followed, "Easy, easy, easy—like your feet touching the ground when you step out of bed." And the daughter concluded, "Neither difficult nor easy—the teachings of the dharma on the tips of the ten thousand grasses."

It all depends on what, and how much, we need to work with and work through. We can call it our karma. Whatever it is we consistently hold on to continually re-creates the illusion of a self. You cannot forget the self until you have put to rest all of the self-centered convolutions, subtle or overt, holy or profane. The person who is dealing with a holy past, walking around with palms in gassho, halo around the head, may have just as much difficulty in practice as a person affected by a profane past. Sacredness, too, can be a sticking place. It does not matter whether you cling to a BMW or the dharma; they both separate you from the truth. In a sense, there is no distinction between holy and unholy. Both create karma that needs to be transcended before we can realize ourselves. That is why true realization is so rare.

So, "practice good." Go by yourself and you will meet it everywhere. It is just you yourself. And yet, you are not it. If you see it in this way, you can be as you are and always have been—perfect, complete, lacking nothing. That is the life of all Buddhas. That is the life of all sentient beings—my life and your life. When we realize that truth, we make it our own.

CHAPTER 8

The Third Pure Precept:
Actualizing Good for Others

Without the moral and ethical teachings, there is no true Buddha-dharma. Without Buddha-dharma, there are no true moral and ethical teachings. Enlightenment and morality are one reality. This statement has perturbed people over the ages and given rise to misunderstandings and concerns that until we are enlightened, we remain immoral. We need to understand that Master Dogen's statement "There is no enlightenment without morality and no morality without enlightenment" arises directly from his equation "Practice is enlightenment." All sentient beings are already perfect and complete, already enlightened, but for most people that enlightenment has not yet been realized. When we practice, we manifest that enlightenment. Practice is not a means to attain enlightenment but the manifestation of enlightenment itself. When we practice the precepts, we manifest that same enlightenment. The precepts are the definition of the life of a Buddha.

The Three Pure Precepts are "pure" by virtue of their all-encompassing nature. We sometimes refer to them as the unadulterated precepts because they are without defilement. The reason they are without defilement is that they include everything. There is nothing outside of them to stain them. They are absolute. They fill the whole universe. Indeed, they are the whole universe itself.

The basis of the precepts is the absolute basis of reality, the realization of no-self. But no-self does not function in the world, amid the daily turmoil and distractions. How do we make it function? It manifests in a form that is in accord with the circumstances; at the same time, it is not hindered by those same circumstances. Manifested in the world, "actualizing good for others" becomes the life of a bodhisattva.

The third of the Pure Precepts is "Actualizing good for others." The prologue to our koan on this precept states:

God mask, devil mask, appearing without form, filling the ten directions, responding without mind, extending over mountains and rivers, converting gods and liberating humans. Appearing in the vast heavens as well as in a speck of dust. Transformed into the sutras and converted into the oceanic storehouse, delivering inanimate and animate beings, releasing all sentient beings from suffering. This is the body and mind of all Buddhas. This is the body and mind of all sentient beings.

The main case of the koan is as follows: "Actualizing good for others" is neither existent nor nonexistent, neither self nor other, neither emptiness nor form. It has no independent existence. It is just actualization of good for others. Further, we should understand that self and other *are not two entities but one—one reality, interdependent and mutually arising. Understanding in this way, "actualizing good" is a continuum of benefaction that transcends time and space, the embodiment and activity of the ten thousand hands and eyes.*

The first pure precept, "Not creating evil," pertains to the negative side of the Grave Precepts, the prohibitions and restrictions. The second pure precept, "Practicing good," is the positive side. It invites and affirms our involvement. For the Ten Grave Precepts to be functioning smoothly, both sides need to be studied and implemented. When both aspects of the Pure Precepts are working fluidly, we have "Actualizing good for others." "Actualizing good for others" functions with the realization that there is no self or other. It is because there is no self and other that there is "Actualizing good for others." "Actualizing good for others" is the life of a bodhisattva.

Master Dogen spoke of four ways that a bodhisattva acts to benefit all beings, four means of leading sentient beings to freedom. The bodhisattvas use these methods to enable people to do good, to avoid evil, and to follow the Way. The first is "giving," both spiritual and material. The second is "loving words" or "loving speech." The third is "benefiting humans by good conduct of body, speech, and mind." Another way to express that is "service for the welfare of all beings." The fourth is "identity with others," assuming the same form as that of the sentient beings to be benefited, "appearing in vast space or in a speck of dust." The poor help the poor; the homeless help the homeless; the depraved help the depraved; the gods help the gods.

What Dogen emphasized in his teachings on "giving" is the way and the spirit in which the giving takes place. True giving means that the giver and the receiver are one reality. When giving happens that way, it is not about doing good anymore. Often, in order to do good, we subtly need to be better than the person we are helping. We reach down into the decay and help the downtrodden, the less fortunate, the helpless. That is not the practice of a bodhisattva. The bodhisattva does not practice from a distance. He or she is right there with those being assisted, covered with the same mud. They climb out together, because self and other are not two separate entities. The giving of a bodhisattva is effortless and purposeless. There is no payoff, no hidden gold.

The principle of "no payoff" applies to everything we do. Routinely, when we wash the dishes, we do it to have clean dishes. That is the payoff—nice, clean dishes to eat from. We rake the lawn in order to have a clean lawn. We tune up a car to have an engine that is running efficiently. That is one way of doing our tasks—very goal oriented. But there is also another way of doing it. We can wash the dishes simply to wash the dishes, not to have clean dishes, but only and completely to wash them. We can rake the lawn, not to have a clean lawn, but just to rake the lawn. We can tune up a car to tune up a car. We actualize good for all beings, not to be a wonderful person and gain nirvana points, but just to actualize good. To actualize good for others is not to create evil, and to practice good.

About the second way the bodhisattva helps others, Master Dogen said:

Loving speech means that as you meet sentient beings, you first arouse the sense of compassion in your mind and treat them with considerate, affectionate words. It is altogether devoid of any violent and spiteful language. Thoughtful words arise from the mind of loving-kindness, and the mind of loving-kindness has compassion as its seed. Loving speech has the power to influence even an emperor's mind. It is not just to speak only highly of others' strengths and achievements.

In a sense, "loving speech" is easy to use and misuse. Every slick politician and salesman is trained in manipulating words, sometimes sweet words. But where is the speech coming from? What is the intent? Is there anything to be gained? If there is even one iota of ego in it, the speech becomes self-serving. It is only when speech arises from no-self that it can truly be called loving speech. Then it nourishes and heals.

"Benefiting humans by good conduct of body, speech, and mind" or "working for the welfare of all beings" means that we create ways to benefit all sentient beings, whoever they might be or whatever their status. Dogen said:

Commiserate with a turtle in trouble. Take care of the sparrow suffering from injury. When you see the distressed turtle or watch the sick sparrow, you do not expect any repayment for your favor, but you are moved entirely by your desire to help others. Then he added: *Therefore, serve enemies and friends equally, and assist self and other without discrimination. If you grasp this truth, you will see that this is the reason that even the grass and trees, the wind and water, are all naturally engaged in the activity of profiting others, and your understanding will certainly serve the other's benefit.*

These guidelines are not a collection of simplistic rules to be followed blindly. They need to be turned inside out and understood experientially. Sometimes, in taking away, there is giving. A master said, "If you have a staff, I'll give you one. If you don't have a staff, I'll take it away." We need to understand giving from that perspective. Loving speech may on the surface sound harsh—for instance, the monitor in the zendo yelling, "Wake up!" But that shout is not self-serving; it is compassionate. If anger is really expressed for the benefit of others, it is loving anger. The mother who scolds her child playing out on the street is using loving words if she is yelling for the benefit and well-being of that child. A car salesman's obsequious manner perverts loving speech when the flatteries are dispatched to get another model off the showroom floor. Walking around with a smile, patting everybody on the back, saying, "Have a good day," is not the way of a bodhisattva.

Finally, there is "identity with others." Identity with others is nondifference. It applies equally to the self and to others. What you do to others, you do to yourself. How you treat yourself is how you treat others. Self and other are one indivisible thusness, the mutual identity of all things. To realize this is to free oneself of birth and death.

"Giving," "loving speech," "working for the welfare of others," and "assuming the same form as that of various sentient beings to be benefited" are the virtues of Kannon Bodhisattva. Every time a person is suffering in pain and someone comes along to alleviate that suffering, that is a manifestation of Kannon Bodhisattva. The physician aiding someone who is injured; the homeless man helping a drunk who has fallen down and hit his head— these instances are nothing other than the virtue of Kannon Bodhisattva manifested in a particular form. It is the life of each one of us.

Here is the verse on this koan:

> No coming, no going,
> No self, no other,
> Nothing to choose, nothing to discard.
> Endless blue mountains
> Without a speck of dust.

We should appreciate that our coming and going always take place right here, right now. "No coming, no going" includes birth and death. In birth, not a particle is added; in death, not an atom is lost. In arriving, there is no gain; in departing, there is no loss. The Diamond Net of Indra reaches everywhere—past, present, and future. Nothing is excluded. That is why we can say, "No self, no other, nothing to choose, nothing to discard." Where would it go? Where would it come from? "Endless blue mountains without a speck of dust" refers to these very mountains and rivers themselves, each one undefiled, perfect and complete, containing everything.

"Not creating evil," "Practicing good," and "Actualizing good for others" are the Three Pure Precepts upon which all of the moral teachings of the Buddha are based. All of the precepts arise out of them. And what are they? The life of each one of us. We should realize there is no place to put this gigantic body. It reaches everywhere.

CHAPTER 9

The Ten Grave Precepts:
Wisdom Mind

The precepts contain the totality of the teachings of the Buddha-dharma. This is not immediately apparent, and it may take us ten to twenty years of practice before we really see it and actualize it in our lives. But it is all there. Totally engaged and thoroughly appreciated, the precepts continue to be a bottomless source of wisdom, helping us to embrace our full human potential, our Buddha-nature. These precepts are the most complete and far-reaching facet of the dharma I could possibly share.

People inquire about practice. "What is lay practice?" *Kai*—the precepts. "What is monastic practice?" Kai—the precepts. "What is home practice?" Kai—the precepts. "What is the sacred?" Kai. "What is the secular?" Kai. Everything we see, everything we touch, everything we do, our way of relating, is right here in these precepts. They are the Buddha Way, the heart of the

Buddha. The full spectrum of emotions, the love, the compassion, the all-embracing mind of clear wisdom, filling the whole universe—it is all here in these sixteen precepts.

As we study the precepts, we need to be able to understand them from different perspectives. The student needs to see the Three Treasures of Buddha, Dharma, and Sangha in three distinct ways: the abiding Three Treasures, the unified Three Treasures, and the manifested Three Treasures. We then examine each of the Three Pure Precepts from the perspective of those nine ways of seeing the Three Treasures. That amounts to twenty-seven different ways of understanding the Pure Precepts. Then from those nine ways of seeing the Pure Precepts we examine the Ten Grave Precepts, giving us ninety ways of seeing them. The precepts also need to be approached from three different points of view—the literal point of view, the perspective of compassion and reverence for life, and the boundless vista of the one-mind Buddha-nature. That is another thirty perspectives. Adding it all up, we have 147 different ways of seeing the precepts, of turning, digesting, and manifesting them. They are considered that important, and that subtle.

The Three Pure Precepts—Not creating evil, Practicing good, and Actualizing good for others—define the natural order of reality. If you eschew evil, practice good, and actualize good for others, you are in harmony with the myriad dharmas that make up this universe. Not creating evil is "the abiding place of all Buddhas." Practicing good is "the dharma of *samyak-sambodhi,* the way of all beings." Actualizing good for others is "to transcend the profane and go beyond the holy, to liberate oneself and others." Obviously, it is straightforward to acknowledge the Three Pure Precepts, but how do we make them function in our lives? How can we practice them? How do we not create evil? How do we practice good? How do we actualize good for others?

The way to do that is shown in the Ten Grave Precepts, which reveal the precise activity of the Three Pure Precepts. Traditionally, the Grave Precepts were expressed as prohibitions. In our sangha we have included an affirmative expression of the precepts as well. They state both what not to do and what to do. Consequently, they balance passivity with activity, dismantling our tendencies to withdraw from the challenges, the complexities, and the turmoil of modern living.

First Grave Precept: *Affirm life. Do not kill.*

Taking the life of any living being is a violation of the first grave precept. Yet, there is a continuous killing that is taking place. We all take part in it. We kill to sustain our life. The hierarchy of life that is commonly accepted among humans, with us on top of the ladder and cows and cabbages below, is an arbitrary one. Life is life. It is all sacred—the tiniest insect, a carrot, a chicken, a human being. All the food we take is life. That is the way it is on Earth. There are no creatures on the face of this planet that take a meal without doing so at the expense of another life.

To consume life is a characteristic of our biological existence. Because of the intimate appreciation of that fact, the occasion of mindfully receiving food in a formal monastery meal is a profound ritual in our tradition. Its purpose is not to take lightly that which we are receiving. To eat is to receive the sacrament of life. We consume life to sustain our life, and to affirm all life. There is no question that human life should be valued very highly, but at the same time, the life of all beings should be respected and treasured. We tend to snatch away the lives of other creatures too readily, disturbing the balance in the environment whenever it suits us.

Self-centeredness is one sure way to violate any precept. If an act is completed solely for the benefit of oneself, that in itself is a violation. It is deluded. There is no self. It is self-centeredness that creates a uniquely human kind of conflict and violence, violence that is not seen among any other species. What we have done to one another throughout history and what we continue to do to one another is sad, appalling, and terribly deluded. This kind of violence is definitely not in harmony with the self-evident laws of the universe. It continually disturbs the growth and development of the ten thousand things in nature, and it destroys the seed of compassion and the reverence for life that emanate from the Buddha-nature.

Clearly, it is not possible for humans to live without killing. Our immune systems are constantly fending off invading microbes. If our white cells did not kill, we would not survive a day. But the spirit of the first grave precept, from the literal point of view, is to exert oneself totally in observing the precept to the best of one's ability.

From the perspective of compassion and reverence for life, we should be clear that this precept means to refrain from killing the mind of compassion and reverence. Also, and this is a very subtle point, an aspect of observing this precept includes killing with the sword of compassion when necessary. Several years ago I was driving along the highway and a raccoon walked out under the wheels of my car. I ran over it. Looking in the rearview mirror, I could see it on the road, still moving. I stopped the car and went back. It was pretty young, badly crushed, and crying out in terrible pain. My own self-centeredness, squeamishness, and fear prevented me

from taking its life and putting it out of its misery. I could
have just driven the car back over it. But I could not bring
myself to do that. I left it on the highway and drove away.
In so doing, I killed the mind of compassion and reverence for life that was inside me. I violated the precept
"Do not kill" because I did not have the heart to kill that
raccoon. My own feelings were more important than the
agony of that creature.

If you have not yet seen into Buddha-nature, it is
very difficult to understand the precepts from the perspective of Buddha-nature. This is their central pillar and why
it is vital to practice them through faith until there is a
full awakening, a direct firsthand appreciation that they
are the complete expression of the life of a Buddha.

Buddha-nature never dies. The realm of Buddha-
nature is completely beyond dualism. As a result, you
cannot oppose killing and nonkilling against each other.
There is no killing, there is no being killed, and there is no
one to kill. To give rise to the thought "to kill" instantly
violates the precepts from this perspective. The thought
itself is essentially deluded.

Bodhidharma commented on each of the Ten Grave
Precepts. He called them the One-Mind Precepts. In talking about the first precept, he said, "Self-nature is inconceivably wondrous. In the everlasting dharma, not giving
rise to the notion of extinction is called the precept of
refraining from taking life." Master Dogen said, "In
affirming life and refraining from taking life, you allow
the Buddha seed to grow, and thereby inherit the
Buddha's wisdom. Do not destroy life. Life is not killing.
Do not kill life."

There is no hierarchy in understanding the precepts
in these three ways. Their appreciation is not progressive.
In hearing about multiple ways of understanding, there is

an immediate tendency to stratify the teachings, claiming that one way of seeing is more advanced and complete than another. So, we may think that to understand the precepts literally is inferior to understanding them from the one-mind point of view. That is not the case. The precepts and their various applications are totally interpenetrated, interdependent, having a mutual causality. One does not exist without the other. They create a matrix, a moral and karmic matrix.

There is a proper spirit of working with the precepts. We should appreciate that spirit. We can approach them with an intention to absorb them into our being, or we can see them as obstructions that need to be avoided or negotiated. In seeing them as barriers to our freedom, we end up looking for loopholes. We bump up against the precepts and rationalize and justify our actions.

The loopholes will go on forever. The Buddha tried to close some of them during his lifetime. His effort resulted in the lengthy list of rules contained in the Vinaya. When the rule of celibacy was introduced, monastics said, "Celibacy applies only to a man-woman relationship. So, a man-man relationship is permitted." Homosexuality flourished. Rules had to be adapted. One monastic had a sexual relationship with a monkey, another with a dead body. Animals had to be included in the celibacy rule, and corpses. And on and on and on. The rules grew in number as the creativity in breaking them grew.

The attitude of trying to outsmart the precepts reminds me of the way my six-year-old son would react to my disciplinary measures. I remember sitting at the dinner table with my two arguing sons. Fed up with all the noise, I shouted, "Johnny, shut your mouth and eat!" He closed his mouth and poured the food against his tightly shut lips so it ran down his chest. In comprehending the spirit of the precepts, and their relationship to our Buddha-nature, there is no need for all the extra regulations and injunctions. There is simply the freedom of living our life wisely and harmoniously.

Second Grave Precept: *Be giving. Do not steal.*

The verse from Bodhidharma's One-Mind Precepts says, "Self-nature is inconceivably wondrous. In the dharma in which nothing can be obtained, not giving rise to the thought of obtaining is called the precept of refraining from stealing." All of the One-Mind Precepts of Bodhidharma start with the statement, "Self-nature is inconceivably wondrous." That is a direct expression of realization. It is the Buddha-nature's expression of Buddha-nature. Buddha-nature is not mysterious. It is inconceivably wondrous. It is radiant, majestic, subtle, yet clear. It cannot be satisfactorily described in words, ideas, and concepts.

"The dharma in which nothing can be obtained" means that it is not possible to possess anything. We cannot step outside to take hold of it. We already contain everything. To possess something, to obtain something, means to separate oneself from something. From the point of view of realization, everything is unobtainable, including the Buddha Way. That is why we chant in the Four Great Bodhisattva Vows, "The Buddha Way is unattainable. I vow to attain it." We already *are* the Buddha Way. All of our machinations, grabbing, controlling, and dominating; all of our squabbling and struggling to get, to hoard, to take, is an upside-down way of understanding the nature of the universe and the nature of the self. Be giving. Do not steal.

We cannot live in harmony with the ten thousand things if we constantly play with the illusions of taking and stealing. Dogen's teaching on this precept goes, "When mind and objects are not discriminated, the gate of liberation is open." The "mind" means the self. "Objects" mean the ten thousand things. "Not discriminated" means to experience them as one reality. When you experience them as one reality, the gate to liberation is open. That is realization.

Again, we need to understand this precept not only from the one-mind point of view but also from the literal point of view. Do not steal means anything, anytime, anyplace. Constantly let go. Do not grasp.

Sometimes, out of reverence for life and compassion, it is necessary to steal. In a sense, every time I steal away from you something that you are holding on to, I am violating this precept. But from the point of view of compassion and reverence for life, I am maintaining the very same precept. One student might appreciate that the teacher is functioning as a thief, taking away everything that is precious to him or her, and bow in gratitude. Another student might get very angry in exactly the same setting. Either way, karma is still being created. Karma does not differentiate between good and bad. Karma is the force to propagate itself and continue. "Good and bad" are the dualistic reference frame that we apply to it.

Third Grave Precept: *Honor the body. Do not misuse sexuality.*

Misusing sexuality indicates the presence of self-centeredness. There is no regard for anything or anyone else. Keep in mind that these precepts arise in the realm of no-self but are designed to function in the world of dualities.

Essentially, there is no separation, but we interact within a matrix of time and space where there is separation. You and I are the same thing, but I am not you and you are not me. Both of these configurations and expressions of reality are functioning simultaneously.

This precept is not a rule that prohibits sexuality. It is a rule that admonishes boorish and manipulative sexuality, where sexuality is used solely for one's own pleasure and benefits, with total disregard for the other person. Sometimes that is blatantly obvious, as in the case of rape, purchasing sexual favors, or child abuse, but sometimes it is considerably more subtle and equally devastating. When we use sexuality to control people, even without any physical contact, when we flirt in order to get the things that we want, to satisfy our own desires, we violate this precept.

Bodhidharma said, "Self-nature is inconceivably wondrous. In the dharma where there is nothing to grasp, nothing to take hold of, 'not giving rise to attachment' is called the precept of refraining from misusing sexuality." Everything in this whole universe is characterized by interdependent co-origination. Is there a way to grab onto anything, to hold and control it? Yet, we constantly struggle with likes and dislikes. Dogen said, "When the three wheels are pure and clean, nothing is desired. Go the same way as the Buddha."

The three wheels are body, thought, and words, or greed, anger, and ignorance, and refer to the karmic activity of the body. Sexuality involves activity of body, words, and thoughts. All are fundamentally empty. That is the ultimate nature of reality. Yet, we are blinded by illusory, dualistic views that give rise to the persistent emotions of love and hate, clinging and rejection, all of which you can call desire. It is all like a dream.

When one clearly verifies for oneself the nature of the self and the nature of all things, then the dualistic distinction begins to dissolve, and love takes on a whole different meaning, one of no separation. Then the loving and sexual relationship between two consenting and caring people is the dharma of unsurpassed enlightenment. It becomes a wonderful expression, not only of human existence, but of the Buddha-dharma itself. And it is one and the same as the way of all Buddhas—the activity of Buddha, the movement of Buddha, the expression of Buddha.

Fourth Grave Precept: *Manifest truth. Do not lie.*

Master Dogen taught, "The dharma wheel unceasingly turns, and there is neither excess nor lack. Sweet dew permeates the universe. Gain the essence and realize the truth." Bodhidharma expounded, "Self-nature is inconceivably wondrous and the dharma is beyond all expression. Not speaking even a single word is called the precept of refraining from telling lies."

Self-nature cannot be described with words. No matter how hard we try to explain it, we speak a falsehood. How could we possibly explain it? No matter how many times we say the word *bitter,* things do not become bitter. No matter how many times we say the word *fire,* things do not become hot. The word is very different from what it depicts. The word is an abstraction of the reality. It is for that reason that it cannot be explained. It is for that reason that it is inconceivably wondrous. And so it is said of the Buddha that in forty-seven years of teaching he did not utter a single word. Everything is this inconceivably wondrous self-nature.

We tend to look at truth as one side and lies as the

other side. We see two distinct polarities. Or we elevate truth to some sort of absolute constant, as if there were a reference book of truth somewhere in the heavens and all things could be checked against it. What is true and what is false? There are no such bottom-line certainties. Truth and falsity always exist within a specific framework. Our ways of seeing are very different. What is true for one person is false for another.

"The dharma wheel unceasingly turns, and there is neither excess nor lack. Sweet dew permeates the universe." "Sweet dew" is perfection. The dharma wheel is the teachings of the Buddha, and those teachings of the Buddha tend to go beyond our dualistic perceptions of the universe. The wheel of the Buddha's teachings turns endlessly. It was turning before there was a universe, before the aeon of emptiness. It will continue turning after all the galaxies burn into cosmic dust. It revolves through all the stages of creation and destruction. In the spring, a hundred thousand beautiful flowers. In the fall, the blaze of leaves on ten thousand mountains. We laugh, we cry, we get angry, we stumble, we fall. This is the clear speaking, present at all times and in all places. In this expression there is no excess and no lack, only completeness of perfection. It is like the sweet rain falling outside the window. It saturates everything.

In each and every thing there is nothing but truth. And yet it is possible, in the realm of this and that, to express falsehood. Usually when we are expressing falsehood, we are protecting ourselves. When this is a self-centered action, it immediately violates this precept, because the precepts spring from no-self.

Under certain circumstances, if you tell the truth, you are violating the precepts. Someone is critically injured in an auto accident, gasping for breath, asking,

"Will I be all right?" If you say, "No, you are going to die," that person may give up right there. If you say, "You are doing fine," it may be a lie, but it provides hope for the person to work with. Out of reverence for life and compassion, sometimes we lie. But if that lie is to protect ourselves, we violate the precept. From the literal point of view, any lie violates the precept, no matter who it is helping.

But what is the truth? Is it good or is it bad? It depends on where you sit. It depends on your position. It depends on your reference system, your matrix. From the absolute point of view, to even give rise to the thought that there is such a thing as truth or falsity violates the precept. That is what Bodhidharma meant when he said, "Not speaking even a single word is called the precept of refraining from telling lies." An old master once said, "Shakyamuni Buddha, Ananda, and Amidabutsu—the more they lie, the more they are Buddhas. If they spoke the truth, they would be just ordinary people. But if anyone said that truth and falsehood are two separate things, this is also deluded speech." These are two parts of the same reality; one cannot exist without the other.

Fifth Grave Precept: *Proceed clearly. Do not cloud the mind.*

"'It' has never been. Do not be defiled. 'It' is indeed the great clarity." That is Dogen's teaching. Bodhidharma said, "Self-nature is inconceivably wondrous. In the intrinsically pure dharma, not allowing the mind to become dark is called the precept of refraining from using intoxicants." Instead of stating, "Refrain from using intoxicants," we say, "Proceed clearly. Do not cloud the mind." It is a broader statement. How do we cloud the mind? There are many ways.

We live at a time and in a culture where there are multimillion-dollar industries dedicated to the research and creation of products and pastimes solely for the purpose of anesthetizing us from our lives. We do it not only with alcohol but also with drugs. We do it with heroin, crack, and psychedelics. People say, "Don't you do it with coffee and cigarettes, too?" Of course. But there is an enormous difference between taking a puff on a cigarette and filling your lungs with crack. By blurring that distinction and seeing all substances as homogeneous in their effects, we create excuses and justifications for abuse and for interpreting the precepts to our liking and for our convenience.

During the seventies, when Zen first came to America, everybody was getting stoned on "grass" and tripping on psychedelics. For some adventurous users it was a rush to drop acid and go sit at the local Zen center. Very soon, people were confusing tripping and *samadhi.* Yet, the difference between tripping and samadhi is staggering. Trying to do zazen while you are stoned or drunk is like trying to swim the English Channel with an anchor tied around your neck. It cannot be done. The drugs do precisely the opposite of what samadhi does. Samadhi is a single-pointed awareness and the falling away of body and mind. Pot activates and scatters the mind. Psychedelics plaster it up against the wall. There is no connection whatsoever between those drugs and genuine spiritual practice.

The Buddha said that it is wrong to cloud the mind. Ignorance means not to understand the nature of the self. Ignorance means no light. Drugs and alcohol numb or hyperexcite the mind and extinguish the inherent light that is there. We see through eyes that are blinded by selfishness, self-centeredness, and chemical confusion.

Traditionally, this precept said, "Do not introduce intoxicants. Do not make others defile themselves. This is the great awareness." In other words, do not enable others to introduce intoxicants, thereby defiling themselves. "Do not come bearing liquor." If liquor is not introduced, it cannot be consumed.

Buying is imbibing. Selling is causing others to drink. We need to understand it that way. People get very technical and say, "Well, this is a gift, so I drink it. I did not buy it. I am not selling it." We do that all the time, stepping over the spirit of the precepts. We know what their intention is, but we prefer to finagle it according to our own preconceived notions. There are a number of monastics and teachers who drink to obvious excess. They justify their drinking by professing that only in the Hinayana tradition does the precept prohibit drinking liquor. They interpret this precept in the Mahayana tradition as not encouraging anybody else to drink. Well, that misses it.

There are all kinds of intoxicants. How we understand ourselves—all of our ideas based on the dualism of self and other—can be considered intoxicants. They cause the greatest darkness. From the absolute point of view, of course, there is no dualism. There isn't any way to cloud the mind. But in the realm of difference and functioning in the world, there surely is. Just look at the number of deaths caused by people driving while intoxicated.

Sixth Grave Precept: *See the perfection. Do not speak of others' errors and faults.*

In his teachings, Master Dogen points out, "In the midst of the Buddha-dharma, we are the same Way, the same dharma, the same realization, and the same practice. Do not speak of others' errors and faults. Do not destroy the Way." How incredibly true that statement is. Ultimately, you cannot destroy the Way. It has always been here. It will always be here. It reaches everywhere. It cannot be created or destroyed. And yet when we attack one another, causing conflict and turmoil, we cloud the beauty of this life. We cover it with opinions and veil it with confusion.

Bodhidharma taught, "Self-nature is inconceivably wondrous. In the faultless dharma, not speaking of others' faults is called the precept of refraining from speaking of others' errors and faults." The whole universe is this wondrous self-nature. Not a particle is outside of it. It is the true self, the original, bare form of all sentient beings.

Nevertheless, out of reverence for life and compassion, sometimes it is necessary to speak of someone's errors and faults. When you witness a murder and the investigators ask, "Did you see anything?" and you say, "No, I did not. I don't want to speak of anybody's transgressions and imperfections," that violates the precept of not speaking of others' errors and faults.

If you speak of others to inflate your sense of self and to elevate your self-importance, you break this precept. To point out what is wrong with someone else is to place the person below you and create separation. But from the absolute point of view, who is the other? Where is the other? This very body and mind fills the universe. There is no outside, nor other.

In the old days within some spiritual communities, there was an internal rule of not discussing the problems of sangha members with anyone outside the community. Such an attitude, frequently fueled by fear, tended to be a whitewash, a conspiracy of silence. When people were abusing power and hurting others, everybody looked the other way. That is enabling and hypocritical. It is not taking responsibility for the precepts in one's life. But at the same time, there are skillful as well as damaging ways of doing what needs to be done. Attaining the clarity to appreciate that difference and acting accordingly are the key to harmony.

If even the slightest thought of self and other enters into the action, you violate the precept. To speak of others' errors and faults in any way violates the precept. When necessary, speak of others' errors and faults, not to serve the self, but only for the good of others. And then, finally, to even give rise to the thought that there is a self and an other is the most deluded view of all, and it violates this precept. So, "In the midst of the Buddha-dharma, we are the same Way, the same dharma, the same realization, the same practice," for all sentient beings.

Seventh Grave Precept: *Realize self and other as one. Do not elevate the self and blame others.*

This precept addresses the importance of taking responsibility and seeing the futility of blaming. When you realize in your life that cause and effect are one, you realize that what you do and what happens to you are the same thing. To see this clearly is to realize that each one of us is responsible not only for ourselves and our lives but also for the whole phenomenal universe. Whatever happens to this great earth, this universe and its inhabitants, happens to each one of us. It is the same karma. When you realize that, there is no way to avoid taking responsibility for your life. There is no way to blame. There is no way to say, "He made me angry," because you realize that only "you" can make "you" angry. With that realization comes the empowerment to do something about anger.

Master Dogen's teachings on this precept read as follows: "Buddhas and ancestors realize the absolute emptiness and realize the earth. When the great body is manifested, there is neither outside nor inside. When the dharma body is manifested, there is not even a single square inch of earth upon which to stand."

The great body is the body of all sentient beings. It includes the earth and the heavens and the stars and the planets. It contains the whole universe. Because there's nothing outside of it, there's no place to put this gigantic body. What you do to the universe, you do to yourself. What you do to others, you do to yourself.

Bodhidharma said, "Self-nature is clear and it is obvious in the sphere of equal dharma; not making any distinction between oneself and others is called the precept of refraining from elevating the self and blaming others. To even give rise to the notion that there is someone to blame violates the precept. Self-nature is inconceivably wondrous. In the undifferentiated dharma, not speaking of self and other is called the precept of not elevating the self and blaming others."

The minute you give rise to the notion of a self you immediately exclude everything else. I always ask the question, "What is the self?" And I always get the same answer, because there is no other way to respond to it. People say, "It's my body, my thoughts, my memory, my history, my ideas." Clearly, all of those are aggregates of the self. What is the self itself? What is a chair? The answer is legs, arms, back, seat. Those are the aggregates. What's chairness, roomness, treeness? What remains when you remove the aggregates?

There are philosophies that say that when you take away the aggregates, what remains is an essence. There is an essence of a chair. Take away the aggregates and the essence is still there. There is an essence of a room, a tree, a deer. And there is an essence of a self. The essence of the self according to Western philosophy is what we call the soul, atman. The experience of Buddhists—thousands of them, men and women for twenty-five hundred years—has been that when you go beyond the aggregates, what remains is nothing—*anatman*, no self. There never was a self to begin with. It was an idea all along. And it is that idea, that notion of a self, that the Buddha says is the cause of suffering, because you close out everything else. You close out the whole universe. The minute you say, "This bag of skin is me; everything inside it is me and everything outside it is the rest of the universe," you have excluded the whole universe from yourself. And everything you need is out there, and differentiation begins. The ego develops and you need to protect that bag of skin. All sorts of things come up—fear and anxiety, separateness, dualities.

This is why we return repeatedly to Master Dogen's teaching: "To study the Buddha Way is to study the self. To study the self is to forget the self. To forget the self is to be enlightened by the ten thousand things." That is, the whole phenomenal universe. How do you forget the self? Zazen. That statement of Dogen's could be reworded to say: To study the Buddha Way is to study the self. To study the self is to forget the self. And to forget the self is zazen.

What is it that remains when the self is forgotten? People worry about that. Will I be the same? Will I like the same things? Will my friends recognize me? Of course! All you are letting go of is an idea. What is it that remains when the self is forgotten? Everything. The whole universe remains. The only difference is that there is no longer a notion that separates you from it. That simple fact changes the way we perceive ourselves and the universe, and it changes the way we relate to the universe. In a sense, the process of zazen is the process of swallowing the universe.

In his instructions to the chief cook, Dogen wrote: "Fools look at themselves as if looking at another. Realized persons look at others and see themselves. The oneness of self and other is the reality realized by Buddhas. The absence of self and other is the reality realized by Buddhas." So, we can say either all self or all other. It's the same thing. I tell people who are working on the koan Mu to work on it that way: either give yourself up to Mu completely or take Mu and make it yourself. Either way it's the same thing. The only way to see Mu is to be Mu.

Master Dogen continued: "The Buddhas and ancestors have realized the emptiness of the vast sky and the great earth. When they manifest as the great body, they are like the sky without inside or outside. When they manifest as the Dharmakaya, there is not even an inch of earth on which to lay hold." There are three *kayas,* bodies of the Buddha: Dharmakaya, Sambhogakaya, and Nirmanakaya. The Dharmakaya is the absolute body of the Buddha; Sambhogakaya is the body of bliss; and Nirmanakaya is the manifestation of the Buddha in the world. All three bodies, all three *kayas,* are the body of all sentient beings, your body and my body. What we realize is that there are no gaps between self and other.

The emperor once asked the national teacher, "Is there anything I can do for you after your death?" And the national teacher said, "Yes, build me a seamless pagoda." No edges, no gaps. That is the pure Dharmakaya, nothing else. Make for me the pure Dharmakaya with your own body and mind, merge with this great earth and the universe—this is what the national teacher was asking for as his memorial. That seamless pagoda is Mu encompassing the whole universe— isn't it, after all, the complete and total self? Is there room there to elevate oneself and blame others?

We can't practice this precept by suppressing the desire to elevate the self and put down others. We can't practice it by trying to praise others. That, too, accomplishes nothing but separation. This precept is about the unity of self and other. It is about seeing the possibility of realizing that unity. Concealing or transforming deluded thoughts concerning self and other does not reach it. The person who seems to be an adversary, making our life miserable, is nobody but ourselves. The stress we experience in our life is not coming from someplace else; we create it. The sooner we realize that, the sooner we are able to do something about it.

Eighth Grave Precept: *Give generously. Do not be withholding.*

There are many ways of giving generously. This precept is not just about giving money or material possessions. Sometimes giving time and attention, simply being present for another human being or another creature, is the most subtle and effective form of giving—just being there, not saying anything, not asking anything, not teaching, not giving, not receiving. It is an incredibly profound and transformative way of giving. It hinges on knowing when that is the right way to act, trusting the situation to elicit that form of giving.

Sometimes we can give our labor, sometimes our concern, sometimes our love. We give, not because something is going to come back our way or because it is good to give. We give because there is no other choice but to give.

This precept was generally understood as spurring us to refrain from begrudging the dharma treasure, the teachings. In other words, it encouraged us not to withhold the dharma. But what is the dharma? Is love the dharma? Is concern the dharma? Is labor the dharma? Is time the dharma? Of course it is—all of it. What is there outside this incredible dharma?

Bodhidharma's One-Mind Precept says, "Self-nature is inconceivably wondrous. In the all-pervading true dharma, not clinging to one form is called the precept of refraining from begrudging the dharma." We can say that not clinging to one form is the precept of giving generously. The "all-pervading true dharma" means the whole universe. "Not clinging to one form" means not to be seized by neediness or wanting. It means not responding constantly to our persistent refrain of "I need, I need, I need" or "I want, I want, I want."

The myriad of dharmas, between heaven and earth, directly and immediately, are the truth, the inconceivably wondrous self-nature. It is ridiculous to even attempt to be withholding. Withholding what from whom? But if we are caught up in a dream of delusion, of separateness, then we are just a bag of skin, everything else is beyond our reach, and desires and regrets arise all the time. So we suffer.

Master Dogen said, "Let go of it, and you are filled by it." The teaching of this precept says that even one *gatha,* one phrase of the dharma, is the ten thousand things. One dharma, one realization, is all the Buddhas and ancestors. From the very beginning there has been nothing to withhold. One phrase, "Form is emptiness, emptiness is form," or one gatha, *"Gate, gate, paragate, parasamgate,"* is the whole universe. But a gatha or a single phrase of the dharma is also "Good morning," "Boy, it's cold," "How are you?" That also encompasses the ten thousand things, from morning until night, from night until morning, twenty-four hours a day. It is constantly teaching. One dharma and one realization—it is the same thing. Walking, standing, sitting, lying down, is also one realization. Everything is the fundamental realization of the whole universe in its entirety. It is none other than the Buddhas and ancestors; it is none other than all sentient beings. No one is left out, no thing is left out.

Ninth Grave Precept: *Actualize harmony. Do not be angry.*

Bodhidharma said, "Self-nature is inconceivably wondrous. In the dharma of no-self, not postulating a self is called the precept of refraining from anger." Not creating an idea of a self frees us completely from anger. You cannot have anger unless there is a self. There is no boundless and omniscient self somewhere in the sky that created the whole universe, and there is no tangible and limited self that inhabits this bag of skin. All of reality is simply infinite dharmas that arise and disappear in accord with the laws of karma. There is not one thing standing against another.

Dogen's teaching on this precept says, "Not proceeding, not retreating, not real, not unreal. There is an ocean of bright clouds, there is an ocean of sublime clouds when there is no anger." Not proceeding, not retreating, not real, not unreal. When we proceed from the assumption that all things have their own being that is separate and distinct from everything else, we progress and we regress. There is truth and there is falsity. We make demands. We want things to be different. We constantly try to influence and change the course of events to fit our own preconceived notions and satisfy our endless desires.

Anger is incredibly debilitating. We come into practice searching, wanting to take care of our questions and doubts. But we carry into our practice all the baggage that has prevented our life from unfolding harmoniously. The baggage is our entangled conglomeration of ideas and positions that have worked together to cause our suffering. It is the deep-seated conditioning that has stifled us and impinged on the lives of others.

We cover the inherent perfection that is originally there with our self-created notion of separateness. When somebody gets ahead of us in the dokusan line or moves ahead of us in their practice, we feel that we lose ground, and we get angry. But if we understand that there is no distinction between the two of us, we immediately return to accord with reality, and there is no anger. Yasutani Roshi said that in getting angry we actually break all of the three dimensions of the precepts—the literal, the compassionate, and the one-mind.

If there is no self, if the action of anger is not self-centered, the energy and the content of what is being communicated becomes entirely different. The shout "Wake up!" heals. It is not for the zendo monitor's benefit. He or she is awake. It is for the guy that is sitting there, nodding off. There is no self-centered anger in that. There is anger at the loss of opportunity to experience our enlightened nature. It is anger similar to the anger of a mother who scolds her child for running out into the road. It is there for the welfare of the child, not because what the child is doing is going to hurt the mother. Expression of such a concern can have a strong impact.

There is compassion in it and it reaches people's hearts. Sometimes it is a way of healing.

Tenth Grave Precept: *Experience the intimacy of things. Do not defile the Three Treasures.*

The One-Mind Precept says, "Self-nature is inconceivably wondrous. In the one dharma, not giving rise to the dualistic view of sentient beings and Buddhas is called the precept of refraining from reviling the Three Treasures." To give rise to the thought "I'm just an ordinary person" reviles and defiles the Three Treasures and breaks this precept. There are only Buddhas. We tend to build dreams of separateness that eventually become nightmares of alienation and isolation, and then we struggle to awaken from the nightmare we have created. To practice this precept is to wake up: there are only Buddhas.

The Buddha-nature is inconceivably wondrous. Not an atom is left out. Not a particle is outside it. Because there is no outside, there is no inside. Therefore there is no way to defile it. The tenth precept closes the loop. The Sixteen Precepts start off with the Three Treasures and end with the Three Treasures.

Master Dogen's teaching on this precept states, "To expound the dharma with this body is the refuge of the world. Its virtue returns to the ocean of omnipotence. It is inexpressible. Wholeheartedly revere and serve this ocean of true reality." The minute you start talking about it, it is no longer the thing you are talking about.

For me, reviling the Three Treasures also includes creating disharmony in the sangha. The essence of sangha is the virtue of harmony. To introduce disharmony is one of the most serious violations within a community. The only situation in which I can envision expelling somebody from the sangha would be if the person were clearly planting seeds of disharmony. It is the worst kind of defiling of the Three Treasures—the Buddha, the Dharma, and the Sangha. It always, and only, happens when we lock ourselves inside our own ego.

All the precepts are nothing other than the life of no-self. To practice them is to practice the life of no-self. They are specifically designed to function in the world of differences and potential conflicts, in the world of this and that, but they arise from no-self.

In order to practice the precepts, we need to take responsibility for them. To practice the precepts is to be in harmony with our life and with the universe. When Master Dogen said, "Practice and enlightenment are one," he was underlining the fact that zazen, the process undertaken to reach enlightenment, and enlightenment itself are the same thing. They are identical, like form and emptiness. When we sit, we manifest the enlightenment of all Buddhas. In the sitting itself, whether we are realized or not, we actualize wisdom and compassion. The same can be said for the precepts. Buddha and precepts are not two separate things. Precepts are Buddha, Buddha is precepts. Each time we acknowledge that we have drifted off a precept, take responsibility, and return to the precept, we are manifesting the wisdom and compassion of the Tathagata.

We are part of the first generation of Western Buddhists, and we carry a special burden that will not be carried by future generations and was not carried by the past generations of practitioners in Japan, China, and Korea. That unique burden is that what we are doing with our practice, all over the West, is not just the realization of ourselves but is also the historical process of the transmission of the Buddha-dharma from East to West. What we do, how we practice our lives, how we manifest the Buddha-dharma by what we do, tells the whole world about these incredible teachings of the Buddha. It is a tremendous responsibility.

It is because of that responsibility that these precepts are so relevant and valuable in our practice. Their profundity is beyond conception. Their flexibility enables them to fill any vessel that contains them. They are dynamic and alive. They nourish and heal. Please, do not take them lightly. Take them into your heart, and give them life in your life. Whether you have received the precepts formally or not, they are yours when you practice them.

CHAPTER 10

The Precepts and the Environment:
Teachings of Mountains and Rivers

Imagine, if you will, a universe in which all things have a mutual identity. They all have a codependent origination: when one thing arises, all things arise simultaneously. And everything has a mutual causality: what happens to one thing happens to the entire universe. Imagine a universe that is a self-creating, self-maintaining, and self-defining organism—a universe in which all the parts and the totality are a single entity, all of the pieces and the whole thing are, at once, one thing.

This description of reality is not a holistic hypothesis or an all-encompassing idealistic dream. It is your life and my life. The life of the mountain and the life of the river. The life of a blade of grass, a spiderweb, the Brooklyn Bridge. These things are not related to one another. They're not part of the same thing. They're not similar. Rather, they are *identical* to one another in every respect.

But the way we live our lives is as if that were not so. We live our lives in a way that separates the pieces, alienates and hurts. The Buddhist precepts are a teaching on how to live our lives in harmony with the facts described above. When we look at the precepts, we normally think of them in terms of people. Indeed, most of the moral and ethical teachings of the great religions address relationships among people. But these precepts do not exclusively pertain to the human realm. They are talking about the whole universe, and we need to see them from that perspective if we are to benefit from what they have to offer and begin healing the rift between ourselves and the universe.

The Three Pure Precepts, Not creating evil, Practicing good, and Actualizing good for others, are a definition of harmony in an inherently perfect universe, a universe that is totally interpenetrated, codependent, and mutually arising. But the question is, How do we accomplish that perfection? The Ten Grave Precepts point that out. Looking at the Ten Grave Precepts in terms of how we relate to our environment is a step in the direction of appreciating the continuous, subtle, and vital role we play in the well-being of this planet—a beginning of taking responsibility for the whole catastrophe.

The first grave precept is *Affirm life—do not kill.* What does it mean to kill the environment? It's the worst kind of killing. We are decimating many species. There is no way that these life-forms can ever return to the earth. The vacuum their absence creates cannot be filled in any other way, and such a vacuum affects everything else in the ecosystem, no matter how infinitesimally small it is. We are losing species by the thousands every year—the last of their kind on the face of this great earth. And because someone in South America is doing it, that does not mean we're not responsible. We're as responsible as if we are the one who clubs an infant seal or burns a hectare of tropical forest. It is as if we were squeezing the life out of ourselves. Killing the lakes with acid rain. Dumping chemicals into the rivers, so that they cannot support any life. Polluting our skies, so our children choke on the air they breathe. Life is nonkilling. The seed of the Buddha grows continuously. Maintain the wisdom life of Buddha and do not kill life.

The second grave precept is *Be giving—do not steal.* Do not steal means not to rape the earth. To take away from the insentient is stealing. The mountain suffers when you clear-cut it. Clear-cutting is stealing the habitat of the animals that live on the mountain. When we overcut, streams become congested with the sediments that wash off the mountain slopes. This is stealing the life of the fish that live in the river, of the birds that come to feed on the fish, of the mammals that come to feed on the birds. Be giving, do not steal. The mind and externals are just thus, the gate of liberation is open.

The third grave precept is *Honor the body—do not misuse sexuality.* Honor the body of Nature. When we begin to interfere with the natural order of things, when we begin to engineer the genetics of viruses and bacteria, plants and animals, we throw the whole ecological balance off. Our technological meddling affects the totality of the universe and there are karmic consequences to that. The three wheels: body, mind, and mouth; greed, anger, and ignorance are pure and clean. Nothing is desired. Go the same way as the Buddha, do not misuse sexuality.

The fourth grave precept is *Manifest truth—do not lie.* One of the very common kinds of lying that is popular these days is called greenwashing. Greenwashing is like whitewashing—it pretends to be ecologically sound and politically correct. You hear Monsanto Chemical Company tell us how wonderful they are and how sensitive they are to the environment. Exxon tells us the same thing. The plastics manufacturers tell us the same thing. Part of what they are saying is true. You couldn't have a special pump for failing hearts without plastic. You couldn't have an oxygen tent without plastic. Sure, fine, thank you. But stop making plastic cups and plates that are not biodegradable and are filling up the dumps. Another kind of lying is the lying that we do to ourselves about our own actions. We go off into the woods, and rather than take the pains to haul out the nonbiodegradable stuff that we haul in, we hide it. We sink the beer cans, bury the cellophane wrappings under a root. We know we have done it, but we act as if it didn't happen. Gain the essence and realize the truth. Manifest it and do not lie.

The fifth grave precept is *Proceed clearly—do not cloud the mind.* Do not cloud the mind with greed, do not cloud the mind with denial. It is greed that is one of the major underlying causes of pollution. We can solve all the problems. We have all the resources to do it. We can deal with our garbage, we can deal with world hunger, we can deal with the pollution that comes out of the smokestacks. We have the technology to do it, but it is going to cost a lot of money, which means that there will be less profit. If there is less profit, people will have to make do with a little bit less, and our greed won't let us do that. Proceed clearly, do not cloud the mind with greed.

The sixth grave precept is *See the perfection—do not speak of others' errors and faults.* For years we have manicured nature because in our opinion nature didn't know how to do things. That manicuring continues right here, on the shores of our river. We have concluded that the river is wrong. It erodes the banks and floods the lowlands. It needs to be controlled. So we take all the curves out of it, line the banks with stone, and turn it into a pipeline. This effectively removes all the protective space that the waterbirds use to reproduce in, and the places where the fish go to find shelter when the water rises. Then the first time there is a spring storm, the ducks' eggs and the fish wash downstream into the Ashokan Reservoir and the river is left barren. Or we think there are too many deer, so we perform controlled genocide. Or the wolves kill all the livestock, so we kill the wolves. Every time we get rid of one species, we create an incomprehensible impact and traumatize the whole environment. The scenario changes and we come up with another solution. We call this process wildlife management. What is this notion of wildlife management? See the perfection, do not speak of nature's errors and faults.

The seventh grave precept is *Realize self and other as one—do not elevate the self and put down others*. Do not elevate the self and put down nature. We hold a human-centered notion of the nature of the universe and the nature of the environment. We believe God put us in charge, and we live out that belief. The Bible confirms that for us. We live as though the universe were spinning around us, with humans at the center of the whole picture. We are convinced that the multitude of things are there to serve us, and so we take without any sense of giving. That is elevating the self and putting down nature. In this universe, where everything is interpenetrated, codependent, and mutually arising, nothing stands out above anything else. We are inextricably linked and nobody is in charge. The universe is self-maintaining. Buddhas and ancestors realize the absolute emptiness and realize the great earth. When the great body is manifested there is neither inside nor outside. When the dharma body is manifested there is not even a single square inch of earth on which to stand. It swallows it. Realize self and other as one. Do not elevate the self and put down nature.

The eighth grave precept is *Give generously—do not be withholding*. We should understand that giving and receiving are one. If we really need something from nature, we should vow to return something to nature. We are dependent on nature, no question about it. But there is a difference between recognizing dependency and entering it consciously and gratefully, and being greedy. Native Americans lived amid the plenty of nature for thousands of years. They fed on the buffalo when they needed that type of sustenance. We nearly brought that species to extinction in two short decades. It wasn't for food. Tens of thousands of carcasses rotted while we took the skins. It is the same with our relationship to elephants, seals, alligators, and countless others. Our killing has nothing to do with survival. It has nothing to do with need. It has to do with greed. Give generously, do not be withholding.

The ninth grave precept is *Actualize harmony—do not be angry*. Assertive, pointed action can be free of anger. Also, by simply being patient and observing the natural cycles, we can avoid unnecessary headaches and emotional outbreaks. Usually, we will discover that the things we think get in the way are really not in the way. When the gypsy moths descended in swarms one year and ate all the leaves off the trees, so that in the middle of June the mountain looked as if it were in late autumn, the local community got hysterical. We made an all-out attack. Planes came daily and sprayed the slopes with chemicals. People put tar on the bases of trees to trap the caterpillars. The gypsy moths simply climbed up, got stuck in the tar, and piled up, so that others crawled across the backs of the dead ones and went up the trees to do what they needed to do. Amid all of these disasters, with the leaves gone and the shrubbery out of the shade, the mountain laurel bloomed as it had never bloomed before. I had no idea we had so much mountain laurel on this mountain. However, the gypsy moths definitely damaged the trees. The weak trees died. By the time July came around, there were new leaves on the trees, and the mountain was green again. But the anger and the hate we felt during those spring months was debilitating and amazing. The air was filled with it.

In another incident, the fellow who owned the house that is now the monastery abbacy had beavers on his property. They were eating up his trees, so he decided to exterminate them. A neighbor told him that they were protected, so he called the Department of Environmental Conservation. The authorities trapped and removed the animals. When we moved into the house, however, a pair of beavers showed up and immediately started taking down the trees again. In fact, they chomped down a beautiful weeping willow that my students presented to me as a gift. I was supposed to sit under it in my old age, but now it was stuck in a beaver dam, blocking up the stream. With the stream dammed, the water rose and the pond filled with fish. With the abundance of fish, ducks arrived. That brought in the fox and the osprey. Suddenly the whole environment came alive because of those two beavers. Of course, they didn't stay too long, because we didn't have that much wood, so after two seasons they moved on. Nobody was taking care of the dam. The water leaked out and the pond disappeared. It will be like that until the trees grow back and the next pair of beavers arrive. If we can just keep our fingers out of it and let things unfold, nature knows how to maintain itself. It creates itself and defines itself, as does the universe. And, by the way, the weeping willow came back, sprouted again right from the stump. It leans over the pond watching me go through my cycles these days.

The tenth grave precept is *Experience the intimacy of things—do not defile the Three Treasures.* To defile is to separate. The Three Treasures are this body and the body of the universe, and when we separate ourselves from ourselves, and from the universe, we defile the Three Treasures.

To practice the precepts is to be in harmony with your life and the universe. To practice the precepts means to be conscious of what they are about—not just on the surface but on many levels, plumbing the depths of the precepts. It means being deeply honest with yourself. When you become aware you have drifted away from the precepts, just acknowledge that fact. That acknowledgment means to take responsibility for your life; taking responsibility plays a key role in our practice. If you don't practice taking responsibility, you are not practicing. It is as simple as that. There is nobody checking when you are doing zazen, whether you're letting go of your thoughts or sticking with them. It has to do with your own honesty and integrity. Only you know what you are doing with your mind. It is the same with the precepts. Only you know when you have actually violated a precept. And only you can be at one with that violation, can atone. To be at one with it means to take responsibility. To take responsibility means to acknowledge yourself as the master of your life.

To take responsibility empowers you to do something about whatever it is that's hindering you. As long as we blame, as long as we avoid or deny, we are removed from the realm of possibility and power to do something about our lives. We become totally dependent upon the ups and downs that we create around us. There is no reason that we should be subjected to anything when we have the power to see that we create and we destroy all things. To acknowledge that simple fact is to take possession of the precepts. It is to make the precepts your own. It is to give life to the Buddha, to this great earth, and to the universe itself.

CHAPTER 11

Verse of the Kesa:
The Robe of Liberation

Each morning after dawn zazen, practitioners in Zen centers around the world chant the Verse of the Kesa:

> *Vast is the robe of liberation,*
> *A formless field of benefaction.*
> *I wear the Tathagata's teaching,*
> *Saving all sentient beings.*

The robe of liberation is the Buddha's robe. The type worn by monastics is called a *kesa,* and the type worn by lay practitioners is called a rakusu. A kesa is worn draped across the left shoulder and wrapped around the whole body. The rakusu is a piece of cloth shaped like a bib, which hangs around the neck. We should realize, however, that the truth of the Buddha's robe is not to be found in any place or in any thing. It is not made of fiber or cloth. It does not possess form, nor is it formless.

Because it reaches everywhere, it is vast. There are no edges or corners to it. Because it reaches everywhere, it is liberating. It is free because there are no boundaries; there are no separations, no gaps. It is one great continuum of interdependence—a formless field of benefaction.

Formlessness has to do with nonduality. Out of that nonduality arise the healing powers of the robe. Its benefits touch all beings—whether one is wearing it or not. When we wear the Tathagata's teachings, we come in contact with the ultimate nature of reality. The Tathagata's teaching means the Buddha's teaching, but it also means the teaching of suchness, the teaching of this very moment. It is the vital experience of the moment that feels missing from so many of our lives. If we miss the moment, we miss our life. It is that important.

Master Dogen in his fascicle on the kesa in the *Shobogenzo* said:

The kesa in which all the Buddhas have taken refuge is known as a symbol of the Buddha-mind and body. It is also known as the robe of detachment, good fortune, no form, perseverance; as the robe of the Tathagata, great compassion, mercy, transcendence of evil; and as the robe of supreme enlightenment. It is the personification of Buddhism. Treat the kesa at all times with utmost respect and reverence and in no way alter its form.

Where does that great power of the rakusu or kesa come from? The Buddha in speaking to one of his monastics said:

When all the Buddhas in the three worlds, pratyeka-buddhas, shravakas, *and all the pure monastics wear the kesa, they are together on the same seat of detachment, hold the same sort of wisdom, overcome covetousness, and enter the same nirvana. Listen carefully. The Buddha's kesa has ten most wondrous merits. The Buddha's robes protect us from embarrassment and cause endless joy. They protect us from extreme temperature and poisonous insects and enable our Buddha-seeking mind to grow. Finally we will realize enlightenment. They give instant recognition of a true practitioner and free us from all forms of greed. They destroy the five wrongful views and assist in good practice. [The wrongful views are belief in a self, holding extreme views, holding false views, attachment to hearsay, attachment to wrong practices.] Acknowledge and venerate the kesa, the symbol of enlightenment.*

My disciple, think of your kesa as you would of a Buddhist stupa, for this causes great joy, purges the mind of evil, and leads both humans and celestials to realization. True practitioners are diligent and respectful. They conduct themselves appropriately to their role and remain unsoiled by delusion and evil. All the Buddhas praise the kesa like they would a fertile paddy, for it is the greatest bestower of peace among celestials and humans. The kesa is endowed with miraculous powers, for it can plant the seed of enlightenment. It helps the new sprout of the Buddha-seeking mind to flourish like the spring plant in a fertile paddy.

The results of Buddha's practice are like a harvested crop in autumn. The power of enlightenment protects like armor made of diamond and we are safe from the poisons of delusion. I have given a brief account of ten most wondrous virtues of the kesa. Though enough can never be said and I could continue for an eternity, if a dragon has an occasion to merely hold a thread of the kesa, he will be protected from being devoured by the garuda bird. Those who cross vast oceans need wear only a piece of the kesa to be protected from the perils. When the great thunderstorms shake the heavens, have no fear. A lay practitioner

*who wears the kesa will keep all evil at bay and, having
perceived the way, received the precepts, and relinquished
the world, will cause the palaces of all the demons to
shake, and that person will soon emerge in the body of
true form.*

How does all this wonderful magic take place with
the rakusu and the kesa? It all has to do with mind—our
mind, no mind, *mushin. Mushin* is Buddha-mind, the
enlightened mind. During the week that precedes jukai,
students who will be receiving the precepts sew their first
rakusu. Each stitch is made by hand, and with each stitch
the practitioner chants, "Being one with the Buddha,
being one with the Dharma, being one with the Sangha."
Each stitch that goes into the rakusu creates a way of seeing and relating to it.

Wearing the Tathagata's teachings, we save all sentient beings from suffering. In Mahayana traditions, practice always comes down to this point. Practice is not just
about self-liberation but is the practice of liberating all
beings. When we place the rakusu on our head while
chanting the Verse of the Kesa each morning, we remind
ourselves of how we practice our life and what our practice is about. It is not just about ourselves. It is about
relieving the suffering of all life, not just our own personal suffering.

The kesa goes back in history to the time of the
Buddha. When someone was leaving home to become a
wandering mendicant, he or she would strip naked, abandoning all possessions. Then the person would sew a garment from fragments of cloth taken from corpses and dye
the cloth yellow with a pigment made from the saffron
plant. This was the mendicant's only garment. The only
other possession was a bowl used for begging and eating.
This was the practice of several yogic traditions in India.

The Buddha followed the custom of the time and wore a simple robe, what we now call the kesa.

When the dharma went to China, the robe symbolizing the mind-to-mind transmission between successive generations went along. In China the climate was much more harsh, and the kesa became an outer garment worn over a warmer layer of clothing. This practical style was continued in Japan, Korea, and Vietnam. The kesa was, and continues to be, used not only by the Mahayana Buddhists but also by the Theravadin and Pure Land Buddhists. It is a symbol of the Buddha's teachings.

Master Dogen said that the kesa must be made of discarded materials that are considered worthless by most people. One should never make a kesa with valuable cloth like silk or brocade. It should not be fancy. But if someone gives you a kesa—even though it is most exquisite and expensive—if the giving is pure, that purifies the kesa.

When Dogen went to China, he was looking for teachings he felt were lacking in the Buddhism of his time in Japan. He had studied Tendai Buddhism and was not satisfied with it. He had entered Eisai's monastery, studied Rinzai Zen with Myozen, and received the transmission, but still he was not content. Then he made the arduous pilgrimage to China. At first he was unhappy there, sensing the same superficiality that he had encountered in Japan. He felt that the dharma had been somehow diluted and that there were no true teachers remaining. He was ready to give up his search when he met a cook who impressed him with his diligence and spiritual insight. He followed the cook to the monastery of Ju-ching. There he studied with Ju-ching, received the transmission, and returned to Japan carrying Ju-ching's lineage, in addition to the one he already had.

Commenting on his experiences at Ju-ching's monastery, Dogen said:

When I was training at a temple in Sung China, I noticed that at the end of each morning zazen session the monastic sitting next to me would place his kesa on his head and with hands in gassho chant the following verse:

How magnificent this robe of detachment
Like a field expounding endless joy and happiness.
Venerating the Tathagata teaching
We vow to save all sentient beings.

When I saw this, I was deeply moved. My collar became wet with tears of joy. Although I had read the Agama Sutra many times and the verse relating to placing the kesa on one's head was familiar to me, I had been ignorant of the manner in which it was to be done. I was sad that there had been no one in Japan to show me this and I lamented at time lost when it was unknown to me. Now, however, as a result of past action, I have been able to witness it. Surely if I had remained in Japan, such an opportunity would not have arisen and the true meaning of the Agama Sutra would have remained unknown to me. With mixed feelings of sadness and joy, I cried the tears, wetting my kesa. At that time I vowed to myself: unworthy as I am, but out of deep compassion, I vow to receive the right transmission of the Buddha's dharma so that my fellow citizens may have an opportunity to experience the true dharma that has been transmitted together with the kesa. This wish was actualized and many lay and ordinary people now wear the kesa. Those who do so should respect and venerate it at all times, for its merit is supreme among all things. With a correct mind, it is not difficult to experience the true word. Even the trees and stones are our teachers. Experiencing the merit of the kesa of right transmission for even a single day or night is the most precious occurrence in our lives.

CHAPTER 12

Lineage of the Ancestors:
Endless Circle

The lineage chart that a student receives during the jukai ceremony is a gesture of unity with the ancestors who have preserved this practice and transmitted the precepts. When students receive the precepts, they are acknowledging that they are entering a continuum—the lineage of ancestors that begins with Shakyamuni Buddha and goes down through the successive generations to the present time.

The chart itself is patterned after the formal document that is used in the transmission of the precepts ceremony, an integral part of dharma transmission at the end of formal training as it is carried forth in the Soto school. During transmission, the disciple does a lineage chart by hand, copying the teacher's lineage on a large piece of silk. Then that lineage is verified by the teacher and transmitted to the disciple who is becoming a teacher in his or her own right. During the jukai ceremony, the student receives a smaller version of this chart prepared for the student by the teacher.

The tradition of the lineage chart dates back to the sixth ancestor, Hui-neng. It was passed through Tung-shan, reached Ju-ching, and was transmitted to Dogen while he was studying in China. Sometime after the chart reached Japan, a variation of it began to be used during the ceremony of receiving the precepts.

The significance of receiving the lineage chart is that it helps make conscious the identity of the life-stream of the Buddhas and ancestors and the life-stream of all sentient beings. The chart is saying that the life of the Buddhas and ancestors and our lives are identical.

The chart is also part of the process of invocation, of invoking the precepts, the lineage of the ancestors, the Buddha. When we are invoking, we are causing something to occur, we are putting it into effect.

With this lineage chart we are invoking all of the Buddhas and ancestors who have preceded us. We are making their life and our life one life by virtue of our vows. If we are going to invoke the Buddha, we have to do it right. Unless we understand what invoking means, we will do it wrong, and if we do it wrong, we will waste our time and never get anywhere with it. We have to really get inside invoking, with the whole body and mind.

In our liturgical services, we chant the names of the Buddhas and ancestors on the lineage chart. Chanting is one thing; invoking is another. Naming is one thing; realizing it, manifesting it, actualizing it, is quite another. Chanting and invoking are worlds apart.

At the very top of the Buddhist ancestral lineage chart is a circle that stands for unity, the pure Dharmakaya. In Zen, the circle is a symbol of simplicity, infinity, and emptiness within fullness. It represents intrinsic oneness and is called the "jeweled mirror of samadhi." It is the eighth stage of practice—complete realization, the full moon of enlightenment. In Zen painting, some of the circles are perfectly round, some of them are lopsided; some are smooth, some broken. Each is perfect and complete.

The Dharmakaya is one of the three bodies of the Buddha. The other two are Sambhogakaya and Nirmanakaya. Dharmakaya is the dharma body of the Buddha and is the fundamental principle prior to the creation of the universe. It is the mind-ground of the equality of the dharma world, which is essentially empty of all characteristics, the dwelling place of all Buddhas of the three worlds of past, present, and future. It is the deep abyss and innermost place of the successive ancestors. It is the way of all sentient beings, whether they have realized it or not. Ordinary beings and sages return to this pure Dharmakaya equally. It has unceasingly continued from ancient times until now. That is why it is sometimes called "the unceasing blood lineage, the great matter of the lifestream."

Out of the pure Dharmakaya circle emerges the name of Shakyamuni Buddha. And from Shakyamuni Buddha it goes to Mahakashyapa. Then it proceeds to Ananda, and so on, from generation to generation. The names are written vertically and the line passes down and up, and down and up again, and then it goes on to the next line, unbroken through the generations of ancestors in India, the generations in China, through Dogen Zenji to Japan, and then through the generations of Japanese ancestors. Finally it comes down to the name of the preceptor. After the name of the preceptor, the name of the student receiving the precepts is written. Then the line continues, returning back into the circle of pure Dharmakaya. It disappears back into where it arose.

The line is usually red because it represents intimacy akin to a blood connection. It is as vital as our genetic connections. If the line were to be stretched out, it would form one huge, continuous circle. When students receive the precepts, in a sense they are saying, "That chart is my life. That is the way I want to live and practice my life. That is my intention in receiving these precepts—my deepest vow." They place themselves in the circle. That circle is the very body that has no beginning and no end. It is also the expression of the unceasing flow of the blood lineage.

When the chart is folded, it is folded in a particular way so that both ends of the chart touch and merge. At the point of juncture, the teacher places the Chinese character for "meeting, matching, or unifying," which brings and seals together the entire chart.

When we receive the chart, we place ourselves in the lineage and make a vow to live our life in accord with the precepts that have been handed down. We vow to make them alive in our own life, to practice them and to maintain them. It is in that practice, that vow, that deep commitment, that we bring the life of the Buddha and the ancestors into our own existence.

CHAPTER 13

Dharma Name:
Spiritual Identity

During the ceremony on receiving the precepts, besides the sixteen precepts themselves, there are three other things that are given by the preceptor and received by the recipient. These are the dharma name, the miniature version of the Buddha's kesa called the rakusu, and the ancestral lineage chart.

The custom of receiving a spiritual name at some point during one's life is common and pivotal in just about every civilization, culture, and religion. We find it among the Native Americans, the Bushman hunters, and the aborigines. We find it in every major world religion— Taoism, Confucianism, Buddhism, Christianity, Judaism, and Islam. Receiving a new name is a rite of passage. It marks an entry point into a particular religious territory. It may involve taking special vows, studying commandments, performing sacred rites, or accepting the precepts of that religion. Whatever the details of the custom, the new name marks a transition and provides a clean slate.

I remember receiving a new name when I was confirmed as a Catholic. At that time I got to pick my name, and I formed a strong and lasting identification with it. It provided a different identity for me, one that was more spacious and hopeful. I liked it so much that I began using it as my second name, rather than the second name given me at birth.

A similar process unfolds in receiving a dharma name. When I pick a dharma name for a student who is about to receive the precepts and is consciously deepening the study of the Way, I spend a lot of time considering it. This is not an arbitrary process. I look at my relationship with the student, the personality of the student, the direction a student is going, and the quality of the student's practice. Sometimes the name is used as a way of indicating what that student's practice needs to be. Sometimes it is an indication of what that student's practice already is.

Dharma names are usually "dharma words," words that have a special connotation in Buddhist practice. Such words are not necessarily words that are in common usage in the Chinese or Japanese language. Usually, Chinese- or Japanese-speaking people, seeing these characters, will interpret them in a conventional way, unless they are practicing Buddhists.

Here in the West, a few Zen teachers have experimented with different ways of creating new dharma names. One teacher has fused Western names with dharma words, so that people can feel more identified with their new name and at the same time keep some sentiment of the dharma. Sometimes Sanskrit names were used to move away from the excessive, and frequently empty, Chinese and Japanese connections. With the Zen

Mountain Monastery sangha I have thought of using Western biblical names, but the images that surfaced were Judeo-Christian, eliminating the possibility of using the teachings contained in the dharma words. I also considered simply employing the English translation of the Oriental words. That ended up at times sounding trivial or idiosyncratic. For instance, my name, Daido—the Great Way—reminded people of a supermarket.

After experimenting, I finally decided to remain with the Chinese characters, so that now the names students receive echo the names of the ancestors in the lineages that have been handed down to us from Tang dynasty China.

Our birth names push our buttons very effectively. They are like a password, an access key into a tightly woven web of conditioning that goes back to our birth. When our name is called, our past comes up. You see this particularly clearly when you address someone by a nickname or a name that he or she was known by as a child. The person may immediately shift posture and attitude, assume a special mode that parallels that name.

A dharma name becomes a koan if approached with the right state of mind. It is an opening, a gate. A new dharma name does not have any sense of personal history. We begin to create our history with it. Rather than plugging in to the habitual syndrome that we manifest in terms of who we are supposed to be or what our conditioning is, we can begin to relate to the sound of our name in a very different way. We do not have the old reference system to fall back on anymore. It opens up a whole new possibility, a whole new way of practicing.

The dharma name becomes a way of seeing yourself. And that is the name that goes on the lineage chart that you also receive during the precepts ceremony. Your dharma name becomes a part of the great unbroken circle representing the Dharmakaya, the pure continuum that begins with the Buddha and ends with the Buddha.

CHAPTER 14

The Four Great Bodhisattva Vows:
Meticulous Effort

Sentient beings are numberless; I vow to save them
Desires are inexhaustible; I vow to put an end to them
The dharmas are boundless; I vow to master them
The Buddha Way is unattainable; I vow to attain it.

Shu jo mu hen sei gan do
Bon no mu jin sei gan dan
Ho mon mu ryo sei gan gaku
Butsu do mu jo sei gan jo.

In Mahayana Buddhism the Four Great Bodhisattva
Vows are the embodiment of our practice, an expres-
sion of a bodhisattva's wisdom and compassion.
Wisdom and compassion are inseparable. Wisdom is the

realization of the nature of the self and the universe. Compassion is the manifestation of that wisdom as the activity of the universe itself. This compassion keeps the bodhisattva functioning in the world. These vows are recited, reflected upon, and embraced every day by Zen students. They are the intent of our lives.

In tracing the history of the four vows, we see that they are as old as Mahayana Buddhism itself. They appear in the Lotus Sutra and in the Prajnaparamita Sutra. They first began to surface some three hundred years after the death of the historical Buddha. In the latter part of the sixth century, Chih-i, the founder of the T'ien-t'ai school of Buddhism, evidently used the four vows in the form we chant today. They are also included in the Platform Sutra of the sixth ancestor, Hui-neng.

In the Platform Sutra there is a description of Hui-neng giving the precepts to a group of lay practitioners. The four vows are a part of the precepts as he taught them. In our lineage we trace the transmission of the precepts to Hui-neng and maintain his form of presenting them along with the four vows.

The audience addressed by Hui-neng was evidently very unusual. It was made up of scholars and government officials—very learned, "upper-crust" practitioners. Hui-neng began the ceremony by having them all recite together the Gatha of Atonement. After completing this "formless repentance," he said:

Learned audience, having repented of all our evil karma, we will take the following four all-embracing vows.

We vow to deliver an infinite number of sentient beings of our mind.

*We vow to get rid of the innumerable defilements in
our own mind.*
*We vow to learn the countless systems of dharma of
our essence of mind.*
*We vow to attain the supreme Buddhahood of our
essence of mind.*

From a Buddhist point of view, all things are nothing
but phenomena in the mind. We create the ten thousand
things with the six consciousnesses. "Essence of mind" is
a term that Hui-neng used frequently, and it refers to the
nonabiding mind. It is the mind that does not abide anywhere—it does not attach to or hold on to the ten thousand things. Ultimately, essence of mind is the true nature
of the mind; it is self-nature, Buddha-nature, enlightenment itself.

Hui-neng continued his teaching:

*All of us have now declared that we vow to deliver
an infinite number of sentient beings; but what does that
mean? It does not mean that I, Hui-neng, am going to
deliver them. And who are these sentient beings within
our mind? They are the delusive mind, the deceitful
mind, the evil mind, and suchlike minds—all these are
sentient beings. Each of them has to deliver himself by
means of his own essence of mind. Then the deliverance
is genuine.*

*Now, what does it mean to deliver oneself by one's
own essence of mind? It means the deliverance of the
ignorant, the delusive, and the vexatious beings within
our mind by means of right views. With the aid of right
views and prajna wisdom, the barriers raised by these
ignorant and delusive beings may be broken down, so
that they are each in a position to deliver themselves by
their own efforts. Let the fallacious be delivered by*

rightness, the deluded by enlightenment, the ignorant by wisdom, and the malevolent by benevolence. Such is genuine deliverance.

As to the vow "We vow to get rid of the innumerable evil passions in the mind," it refers to the substitution of our unreliable and illusive thinking faculty by the prajna wisdom of our essence of mind.

As to the vow "We vow to learn the countless systems of dharma," there will be no true learning until we have seen face-to-face our essence of mind, and until we conform to the orthodox dharma on all occasions.

As to the vow "We vow to attain supreme Buddhahood," when we are able to bend our mind to follow the true dharma on all occasions, and when prajna always rises in our mind, so that we can hold aloof from enlightenment as well as from ignorance and do away with truth as well as falsehood, then we may consider ourselves as having realized the Buddha-nature, or in other words, as having attained Buddhahood.

Learned audience, we should always bear in mind that we are treading the path, for thereby strength will be added to our vows.

When Hui-neng is asking about the beings in our mind, what is he talking about? Are the "delusive mind, the deceitful mind, the evil mind, and suchlike minds" just things we think about? Or is he talking about people—people who are delusive, deceitful, or evil? When we think of saving sentient beings, we always think of somebody who is down-and-out, who needs to be saved: the homeless, the hurt, the walking wounded. How about those who do not fall into those categories? Somebody who is deceitful is not very lovable, maybe not even approachable, yet such people are sentient beings. Many of the very powerful people in this world, the movers and shakers, are the sentient beings who need saving. We save them and we save everything that they are touching, everything that they are affecting. This is reflected in one of the modern translations of the first vow, phrased, "Creations are numberless; I vow to free them."

In Buddhism we understand reality to be created with our minds, with our consciousness. In the coming together of the organ of perception, the object that it perceives, and consciousness, reality is established. If we remove any one of these three components—the organ, the object, or consciousness—it no longer exists.

The way we release reality from consciousness is through the practice of deep meditation. The realized emptiness, though, is just one side of totality. There is another side—form and its very real existence. Again and again, throughout the teachings, we are shown that the truth is in neither of these extremes. That the form is empty is the experience of *shunyata,* the experience of the pure Dharmakaya, the absolute basis of reality. It is the breakthrough of *kensho.* What follows that realization is that emptiness is form. Without an appreciation of the relative, we would be like zombies, walking around bumping into walls, with "no eye, ear, nose, tongue, body, or mind." The truth of our practice is neither in emptiness nor in form. Then where will you find it? This is neither "a book" nor "not a book." Then how will we define it? It cannot be expressed with speech or silence. When Hui-neng says, "Who are these sentient beings within our mind," in what realm is he?

"They are the delusive mind, the deceitful mind, the evil mind and suchlike minds—all these are sentient beings." When Buddha was sitting under the bodhi tree on the night of his enlightenment, he was accosted by

Mara and visited by countless demons: frightening, repulsive, chaotic, seductive forces. He dealt with them one by one and cleared his mind. There are many people who come to dokusan and tell me about their fear of emptiness. They stand on the edge of letting go but are frightened, gripped by the demon called "fear." There are the sexual demons—another way of distracting ourselves from practice. Buddha was visited by naked, dancing women. There are women practitioners who are visited during their meditation by naked, dancing men. There are demons of anxiety, of anger, of confusion, and all of them are creations of the mind. You deal with them by dealing with your mind.

"With the aid of right views and prajna wisdom, the barriers raised by these ignorant and delusive beings may be broken down." What is the right view and the wisdom that allows the barrier to be broken down? It always comes back to *Be the barrier.* That is the right view. *Be the barrier.* That is the wisdom. This is because, from the very beginning, the barrier is nothing but yourself. There is no barrier. When you realize there is no barrier, the barrier becomes a dharma gate. If the barrier is Mu, be Mu. If the barrier is the koan, be the koan. Anxiety? Be the anxiety. Fear? Be the fear. When you are the barrier, it fills the universe. There is no place that it does not reach—and that is identical to no barrier. There is no longer a reference system. There is no separation—no self and other, no self and barrier, no self and Mu, no self and the koan, no self and the breath.

The phrasing of the four vows is very subtle and rich. It represents centuries of evolution through culture and language. There are several translations and many interpretations. From the scholarly point of view, the variety is partially due to the nature of Chinese written characters, which carry multiple meanings and nuances. From the dharma point of view, these four lines are the distillation of the bodhisattva ideal. The four vows are not just some kind of prayer; they are not a simple chant. They are an essential koan. They contain the totality of the scriptures, records of the masters, all of the koans, and the sutras themselves. All of the voluminous Mahayana literature can be reduced to these Four Great Bodhisattva Vows. Do not take them lightly. They are the life of the Way—your life and my life.

The First Vow

Sentient beings are numberless; I vow to save them.
Shu jo mu hen sei gan do.

Shu jo mu hen sei gan do. The character *shu* means "all" or "many." *Jo* means "beings," or it can mean "life." So we have "all the numerous living beings," "the many beings," or "the many lives." *Mu* means "no," "nothing," or "without." It is a negation. *Hen* means "limit," "boundary," or "edge." Putting all that together, we come up with "All beings, all life, are without edges, boundaries, or limits."

Sei gan is repeated in every line and is the turning point of each phrase. Both characters stand for "vow," but they also mean something else. *Sei* can mean "pledge," and *gan* can mean "prayer." It is a prayerful vow, or a prayer-vow, that is being made.

A vow is very decisive. In a sense, it is a resolution. It speaks of intent and commitment. It speaks of action. To vow really means to *do*. To commit means to *do*. When a commitment is present, we do not have to make any more decisions. There is freedom from ambivalence and uncertainty of purpose. When you climb the ladder of a diving board and finally commit to the dive, you are diving. You cannot change your mind and go back up onto the diving board when you are soaring through the air. With commitment, there is no longer a search. That is why we put such an emphasis on commitment. It is all-important.

A vow releases us from the decision-making process. It allows our whole consciousness and all of our energy to be directed into action. When we are committed, we are in the process of doing. We are no longer asking, "Should we do it?" We just do it! This is a totally different state of consciousness from the state of deliberation that precedes it.

There are people who go from the cradle to the grave deliberating. They never make up their minds. I know graduate students who received their Ph.D.'s ten years ago and are still in school taking postgraduate courses. They do not want to get out into the world and confront and embrace their lives. In pursuing and accumulating knowledge, they remain passive. They want to be students for the rest of their lives.

We go through the motions of making a commitment in marriage, but it usually ends up being an empty gesture. In fact, in the latter part of the seventies and the early part of the eighties, the word *commitment* became a dirty word. That attitude is changing, but there is still a great deal of resistance to the concept, as well as to the reality, of commitment. For some reason we insist on seeing commitment as an entrapment rather than the freedom it actually is.

The bodhisattva vow is a prayerful vow. But it is important to understand the nature of "prayer" as it operates in this special context. It is not a term often used in Buddhism, although some translators interchange "vow" and "prayer," particularly scholars who come from the Judeo-Christian traditions. Many of the Catholic priests who have translated Buddhist texts tend to use that word.

Evelyn Underhill, in her book *Mysticism,* talks about orison, or prayer. She enumerates eight levels of prayer, elucidating the difference between the prayer of someone like Saint John of the Cross, for example, and the person in the street going to church once a month. In the latter case the person usually makes prayers of petition. The person wants something from someone who is powerful and separate, namely, God. The other end of the spectrum is the eighth level of orison, the prayer of union, in which there is no separation between the one praying, the prayer, and the one to whom the prayer is directed. There is just complete identification and intimacy. That union is probably closest to the way we would look at the prayerful vow in Buddhism. One has unified with the vow to such an extent that there is no sense of doing. One has no sense of doing something for all sentient beings, because in the state of consciousness of the vow, all sentient beings are none other than oneself.

The first line then declares: "All of the many beings without limit, I pray-vow to save them." "To save them" means "to carry them to the other shore," the shore of realization. This crossing over, the ferrying of sentient beings across the river, is an old Buddhist image. It comes up frequently in the records of the Zen masters. When the fifth ancestor transmitted the dharma to the sixth ancestor, he took him to the river and said, "Cross over to the other side and go on your journey." The sixth ancestor said, "You don't need to row me across. I can do it myself." Still, the fifth ancestor insisted on ferrying him to the other shore. I am sure that this incident is included in the story because of the significance of the metaphor.

If you really understand "other shore" and "crossing over," you understand that *that* shore and *this* shore are the same shore. That shore is the shore of enlightenment; this shore is the shore of delusion. If you really understand the nature of enlightenment and the nature of delusion, you realize the identity of the two. Master Dogen, in his teachings, says, "To cross over to the other shore is deluded. But to say that the other shore arrives is enlightenment." A rewording of this in his *Genjokoan* is slightly more elaborate: "To carry the self forward and to realize the ten thousand dharmas is delusion. That the ten thousand dharmas advance and realize the self is enlightenment."

One would think that to search and advance on the path, realizing its myriad aspects is what enlightenment is about. Dogen flatly rejects that, qualifying such activity as deluded. Dogen always takes dichotomies, whatever they happen to be, and merges them, showing how they interpenetrate and how they are codependent and not hindering each other. "To carry the self" is to look outside the self. Isn't that what all of the ancient pilgrim monastics were doing? Isn't that what the pilgrims of today are doing, running from one teacher to another, carrying the self forward, attempting to realize the ten thousand dharmas? That the ten thousand dharmas advance is the intimacy of the ten thousand dharmas and the self. It is enlightenment.

What Dogen says is that to seek after enlightenment is deluded. Yet, it is very difficult not to seek. We are constantly grabbing at enlightenment, and in that grabbing we separate ourselves from it. The very act of reaching for something is based on separation—you cannot grab for something unless you are separated from it. Immediately, the intention reflects an inherent delusion. We become preoccupied. The desire for enlightenment separates us from enlightenment. The desire to save all sentient beings separates us from sentient beings. That desire is very different from raising the bodhi mind. It is very different from the aspiration for enlightenment. It is different from a vow. One has to do with expectations; the other has to do with moment-to-moment practice.

From the sixth ancestor's point of view, what does it mean to deliver an infinite number of sentient beings? "It does not mean that I, Hui-neng, am going to deliver them." "I, Hui-neng" does not exist for the sixth ancestor. He is not separate from the ten thousand beings. "And who are these sentient beings within our mind? They are the delusive mind, the deceitful mind, the evil mind, and suchlike minds—all these are sentient beings." What he is describing is people in distress. The deliverance is deliverance from suffering. Yet, each sentient being is already perfect and complete, already a Buddha. "Each of them," he says, "has to deliver himself by his own essence of mind. Then the deliverance is genuine." The essence of mind is the nonabiding mind, self-nature, Buddha-nature.

Now, what does it mean to deliver oneself by one's own essence of mind? It means bringing peace to the ignorant, delusive, vexatious beings within our mind by means of right views and prajna wisdom. Wisdom is the realization that all of these creations are a process we engage in. We create the barriers, delusions, and ignorance. We create the joy and the bliss just like we create the pain and the suffering. We are, in fact, the master of our own existence. Hui-neng goes on to say, "They are each in a position to deliver themselves by their own efforts. Let the fallacious be delivered by rightness, the deluded by enlightenment, the ignorant by wisdom, and the malevolent by benevolence. Such is genuine deliverance."

The Second Vow

Desires are inexhaustible; I vow to put an end to them.
Bon no mu jin sei gan dan.

Bon no mu jin sei gan dan. This vow is very closely related to the first. All of these vows are tightly knit and operate together. *Bon* means "troublesome." *No* is the word that is used to describe anxiety, distress, pain, or any form of suffering, and it includes their causes. It is what the Chinese used when they translated the Sanskrit word *klesha*—defilement. Many translators use "greed, anger, and ignorance" as a translation of *bon no*. Chinese Buddhists interpreted it as "delusions" or "temptations." Yet "delusions" is too limited a translation, and "temptations" has a variety of Christian connotations. Some scholars use "passion," but as Aitken Roshi points out, "passion" is misleading because when there is no passion, there is no life. We are not trying to get rid of passions. Probably the best interpretation is the "three poisons": "Greed, anger, and ignorance arise endlessly; I vow to cut them off."

Mu again means "not" or "without," and *jin* means "exhaustible," so *mu jin* means "endless," "boundless," "inexhaustible." Again, *sei gan* stands for "prayerful vow." The character *dan* has been translated as "to extinguish," "to cut," but it should read softer than that. "Put an end to them" is more gentle and deliberate; "cut" is sharp and direct. "Desires are inexhaustible; I vow to put an end to them."

There is a book entitled Zen Dawn, which is a

translation of an eighth-century text discovered in the western part of China. It is one of the earliest records of the Northern school of Buddhism. The book includes a dialogue between Bodhidharma and the second ancestor, Hui-k'o. In it, Hui-k'o asks Bodhidharma, "Why is the contemplating mind called 'complete comprehension?' " And Bodhidharma answered:

When the great bodhisattvas practice profound perfection of transcendental wisdom, they comprehend that the four great elements and the five clusters are fundamentally empty and selfless. They see that there are two different kinds of activity initiated by inherent mind: pure states of mind and defiled states of mind. Pure mind is the mind of undefiled, true thusness. Defiled mind is the mind of defilement and ignorance. These two kinds of mind are both there, of themselves, from the beginning. Though everything is produced by the combination of temporary causes, pure mind always takes delight in good causes, while defiled mind is constantly thinking of evil deeds. If true thusness is aware of itself and, being aware, does not accept defilement, then this is called being a sage. This enables one to leave all suffering far behind and experience the bliss of nirvana. If you follow along with defilement and create evil, you are subject to its bondage. This is called being an ordinary person. Then you are submerged in the triple world, subject to all kinds of suffering.

The second ancestor went on, "You've just stated that all the merits of the enlightened nature of true thusness depend on enlightenment as their root. I wonder, what's the root for the forms of evil mind, the mind of ignorance?" Bodhidharma replied:

Though the mind of ignorance has eighty-four thousand afflictions, sentiments, desires, and unaccountable evils, in essence they all have the three poisons as their root. The three poisons are greed, anger, and ignorance. The mind of these three poisons of itself inherently includes all forms of evil. It's like a great tree: though there is one root, the branches and the leaves it gives life to are numberless. Each of the three poisons as a root gives birth to evil deeds even more prolifically. These three poisons become the three poisons from a single, fundamental essence. They are sure to manifest the six sense faculties, also called the six thieves. The six thieves are the six consciousnesses and they are called six thieves because they go in and out via the sense faculties, becoming attached to the myriad objects and forming evil deeds that block off the true thusness. All sentient beings are plunged into ignorance and confusion by these three poisons and these six thieves. Body and mind sink down into birth and death and revolve through the six planes of existence, receiving all kinds of suffering and affliction. It's like a river that starts from a small spring: since the flow from the source is unbroken, it can extend its waves for thousands of miles. If a person cuts off the root source, then the many streams all stop.

That "cut off" is the key. Cut the roots, and the tree withers and dies.

Bodhidharma said that there are two kinds of mind, both there of themselves from the beginning. We are all very familiar with both of them. Don't we constantly encounter these two kinds of mind in our practice? There is the mind that realizes something is not quite right and that life does not need to be a journey of suffering, pain, and confusion. It is the mind that wants to practice and enters into practice. Then there is the other mind that is saying, "I don't want to do this" "Why am I doing this?" "I'm not going to get involved." These two minds are in a dynamic tension. It is a continuing, back-and-forth struggle.

The Ten Ox-Herding Pictures are a poetic depiction of that process. At first the seeker sees the ox (which represents the true self) off in the distance. It is a moment of direct insight, quickly covered with a flood of intellectual understanding. With time, and after much effort, there is increasing clarity. The ox is taken hold of. But the problem persists as, even after he is gotten hold of, the ox keeps wandering off, doing what he wants. The student has to use the nose ring, holding it tightly and exercising control. That is the struggle. When we get to the fifth and sixth ox-herding pictures, the tension disappears. In the pictures, the herder on top of the ox is playing his bamboo flute, enjoying the sun, riding the ox home. Everything is straightforward and easy. The dichotomy of the two minds is finally resolved.

People come into practice and expect that the process is going to be completed in a weekend. Realizing the self thoroughly does not happen overnight. The struggle can continue for quite a while. It takes a lot of perseverance before the struggle is over. And the end of struggle does not mean enlightenment; it does not mean unobstructed clarity. It may mean seeing the nature of the self, but that is not what we refer to as *anuttara-samyak-sambodhi,* complete realization. That degree of "falling away of body and mind" is portrayed in the eighth ox-herding picture. Still, when the struggle is over, it is a significant step.

Bodhidharma continued: "Those who seek liberation must be able to transform the three poisons into the three forms of pure discipline, and transform the six thieves into the six *paramitas,* thereby leaving behind forever all forms of suffering." How do we take the three poisons and turn them over? When we turn them over, on the other side are the three virtues. Greed, anger, and

ignorance become compassion, wisdom, and enlightenment. The poisons are based on separation. Even the
desire for enlightenment is deluded, because it is based on
there being a separation between the self and enlightenment. Even the desire to help all sentient beings is
deluded. It, too, implies separation. Someone who wants
to help people and becomes a do-gooder, running around
self-consciously "saving all sentient beings," is very different from a bodhisattva who truly embodies compassion.
In compassion there is no sense of separation.

The other side of ignorance, which literally means
"having no light," is enlightenment, having light, seeing
what is real. Actually, that is the bottom line, because
when ignorance is transformed, the other two poisons
transform. If you are trying to advance in darkness, you
keep bumping into obstacles. To realize yourself is to
"turn the light on" and to see the reality the way it is, to
see the self the way it is, to perceive the universe the way
it is. It is to understand the essence of mind, take responsibility for your life, and realize that what you do and
what happens to you are the same reality. The process
and the goal are the same reality. They are not separate.

We transform greed, anger, and ignorance into the
virtues of compassion, wisdom, and enlightenment with
atonement. That is what "at-*one*-ment" means. "All evil
karma ever created by me since of old, on account of my
beginningless greed, anger, and ignorance; born of my
body, mouth, and thought. Now I atone for it all." We
create karma with what we *do* with our bodies, what we
say, and what we *think*. All of that is karma; all the
actions and consequences of our life are karma. When we
manifest anger with our body, just being angry, that is the
karma we create. When we manifest it with our mouth,
that is the karma we create. When we manifest it with our

thoughts, that is the karma we create. The thought of violence is just as violent as the act and the word. It debilitates the person it is directed toward, and it hurts the one thinking it even more. Evil karma creates evil effects. Every cause produces an effect, and that effect is the cause of the next event. The force to continue is tremendous. Once you start the ball rolling, it goes on and on.

How do you turn around this evil karma of greed, anger, and ignorance? "I now atone for it all." I am now at one with it all. To be at one with it all means to take responsibility for it, to acknowledge that we are the creator of it. We acknowledge that anger is not something that happens to us but something that we do. Greed is not an accident—we create it. When we really bring this responsibility home, our life changes dramatically.

It is very easy to justify greed. We do it all the time. That is how corruption in business, politics, and religion continues. But even from a self-centered point of view greed does not make sense. Even a nitwit with a modicum of introspection will see that greed ultimately destroys the greedy. It is based on separation. It disconnects one from the fabric of life. In at-*one*-ment there is no self-centeredness. When we take responsibility for greed, it begins immediately to transform into compassion.

This practice always comes down to intimacy. Intimacy with what? What are we intimate with when we are intimate with anger? What are we intimate with when we are intimate with our own greediness? What are we intimate with when we are intimate with our delusion, distress, anxiety, fear, worry? We are being intimate with the self, with our self. This is why we teach that to forget the self is to really be intimate with the self.

People who do not understand such intimacy misconstrue this process as a New Age form of self-centeredness.

But the self does not exist; it is an illusion. When we are really intimate with the self, the entire phenomenal universe returns to the self. This is studying the self, realizing the self, manifesting the self as the life of the Buddha.

Someone once asked my teacher Maezumi Roshi, "If all beings are Buddha, how about someone like Genghis Khan or Adolf Hitler? Are they Buddhas, too?" What Maezumi Roshi answered was interesting and challenging. He said, "When you start a painting, you have a blank piece of paper, a brush, and ink. With that blank piece of paper, everything is possible. The minute we start painting, we create one of the countless possibilities. That is our life, moment to moment." His point is that the whole spectrum of human existence exists in every one of us. We have the potential to manifest Genghis Khan, and we have the potential to manifest the Buddha, and everything in between. And we do.

We are constantly painting. Life is constantly unfolding. Definitely, my life of thirty years ago is not what my life is today. Everything changes. Each one of us is in a constant state of becoming. Nothing is fixed. That is the most exciting thing about this life. No matter how bad it is, it is going to change. No matter how good it is, it is going to change. And we never know which way it is going to unfold. It keeps the hair on the back of your neck erect. You have to be alert, ready, and open.

This life is a wonderful gift. What a waste if we live it wallowing in distress, anxiety, and fear. That kind of suffering is not necessary. We have the same equipment as all the Buddhas who ever lived, and we have at our disposal this incredible dharma. It is right at our fingertips. The potential is here. In fact, the Buddha is here. Underneath the layers of conditioning, underneath the anxiety, the stress, the greed, the anger, the ignorance, the confusion, lives a Buddha who is nothing other than our life. Zazen is a process for burning off all of this extraneous "stuff" that we identify ourselves with, and that we tend to hate about ourselves. When that is all burned off, there, right where it has always been, is the life of the Buddha. Your life, my life, our life. Just one life.

The Third Vow

The dharmas are boundless; I vow to master them.
Ho mon mu ryo sei gan gaku.

Ho mon literally means "dharma gates." *Ho* means "dharma," and *mon* means "gates." We take these first two words and translate them simply as "dharmas." *Mu* again is a negation: "without" or "no." *Ryo* means "measure" or "amount." So *mu ryo:* "without measure." "Dharma gates without measure."

Sei gan, as before, stands for "prayer-vow," "prayerful vow." And *gaku* means "to study" or "to learn." It can also be translated as "apprehend," "master," "perceive," or "understand." Aitken Roshi elaborates on these terms. About *gaku,* "to study or learn," he says, "to study religion in order to get rid of illusions." And about *ho mon,* "dharma gates," he adds, "the doctrines or wisdom of the Buddha, regarded as the door to enlightenment."

The word *dharma,* just like its sister terms *Buddha* and *sangha,* can be used in several ways. The dharma is the teachings of the Buddha, but *dharma* also means the ten thousand things—the whole phenomenal world. *Buddha* means Gautama, the historical Buddha; it also means the enlightened one. And *sangha* means the community of practitioners, as well as all beings in the whole universe. In a sense, *Buddha, dharma,* and *sangha* mean the same thing, and they all reduce to the same starting point—each one of us.

"The dharma gates are without measure, I vow to study, learn, apprehend, master, perceive, and understand them." Sometimes, in reading these four vows, I like to substitute the word "realize" for the other verbs. It can be applied to any one of the lines: "Sentient beings are numberless; I vow to *realize* them." To not separate from them but to be one with them. "Desires are inexhaustible; I vow to realize them." To cut them off and stop them is to realize them. How do we stop the sound of a temple bell? We stop it by realizing it. "The dharma gates are boundless; I vow to realize them." No separation. Be the dharma gates with the whole body and mind. There are myriads of dharma gates. Mu is a dharma gate. The breath is a dharma gate. The six senses are dharma gates. Each of our barriers is a dharma gate. "Enter there," the vow reminds us, "enter there."

Realization differs from intellectual understanding. To understand something means to "penetrate the word." To realize is to be intimate with the essence of the word. Dogen said, "To realize the essence and not penetrate the word is to have eyes open in darkness." Realization alone is not enough. "To penetrate the word and not realize the essence is to have eyes closed in the bright light of day. To both realize the essence and penetrate the word is to have eyes open in the bright light of day."

The sixth ancestor, speaking of this vow, says: "As to the vows to learn the countless systems of the dharma, there will be no true learning until we have seen face-to-face our essence of mind, and until we confirm the dharma on all occasions." To confirm it is to actualize and manifest it. He also said, "We take the dharma as our guide because it is the best way to get rid of desire."

In a dialogue between the second ancestor and Bodhidharma, Hui-k'o asked, "The sutra says, 'All things come forth from this scripture.' What does this mean?"

Bodhidharma answered: *"Scripture" means mind. Mind can manifest everything. All people who practice develop illumination by cultivating the supreme correct path of unobstructed awareness. All the Buddhas, all the Tathagatas, begin with their own cultivation and end by transforming other beings. There is nothing that they do not achieve. Hence the saying, "All things come forth from this scripture."*

Hui-k'o then asked, "The sutra talks about the Tathagata bearing a load. What does that mean?"

Bodhidharma responded: *You should reflect back on reality nature. Not abiding in your usual state, instead you become aware that you have no permanent body. Who will bear the load? Profoundly comprehending transcendent wisdom and broadly expounding it for people is bearing the load of the true dharma. The Buddhas convey its excellent meanings and that all sentient beings achieve meritorious deeds. Hence, the talk of the Tathagata bearing a load.*

Hui-k'o asked, "What does it mean when the sutra says that the Tathagata delivers sentient beings?"

Bodhidharma said: *You must understand for yourself that the true identity of sentient beings is fundamentally pure. But when the six sense faculties create the vexations of form, sickness is born. When we observe that birth is fundamentally empty, what is there that can be delivered? Therefore, if you say that the Tathagata delivers beings, you are attached to notions of self and others.*

Hui-k'o asked, "How shall we deal with this mind of the three poisons in order to achieve the six paramitas?"

Bodhidharma answered: *You must have courage and move forward energetically toward the three poisons.*

This remarkable dialogue took place around the year 500 C.E. How many people are concerned with the questions it contains? How many people even have the feeling that some essential information is missing about this life? Those who begin a spiritual search ask these questions. It usually begins when we realize that nobody has given us the whole story—in our education, in our spiritual training, in our growing up—something seems to be missing. As we look toward the models our civilization has produced—our scientists, politicians, religious leaders, teachers, parents—they all seem to be caught in the same trap. Where are the answers to be found? Does anybody know what is going on?

For many years, in my own search, I truly believed nobody knew the answers. Philosophers and spiritual leaders were not making any sense. The collective culture was not making any sense. And there was a discrepancy between the lack of explanation and a very deep sense I had that there was a harmony within the totality of this apparent chaos. But how to find it? What is that harmony? My education did not provide a clue. The libraries did not have the answers. The wise ones and the sages of our culture did not seem to address this problem with sufficient depth. So I concluded that nobody knew what was going on.

At the time when I turned to Buddhism, there was very little of it going on in the West. Then, slowly, the migration of teachers and the influx of teachings began. I found out that for thousands of years there have been people in tune with the universe, transforming their lives. By global population standards, they were a handful, but they were genuinely committed to seeking the truth. And what did they say? Take the backward step. Turn yourself inward. Study yourself, forget yourself, realize yourself.

"How should we deal with this mind of the three poisons in order to achieve the six paramitas?" asked Hui-k'o.

Bodhidharma said: *You must be courageous and bold, and advance energetically toward the three poisons. Take the three vows. Vow to cut off all evils to deal with the poison of anger. Vow to cultivate all forms of good to deal with the poison of ignorance. Vow to deliver all sentient beings to deal with the poison of greed. When the ability to cut off evil and the ability to cultivate good come together in the mind, the three poisons are curbed and you achieve the Three Pure Disciplines.*

He is talking about the Three Pure Precepts: Not creating evil, Practicing good, Actualizing good for others. How do we subdue the three poisons? How do we achieve the six paramitas in everyday life, with people and situations that are conflicting and frustrating? We apply the subduing mind toward the five clusters of form, sensation, perception, motivational synthesis, and consciousness, the five conditions that create what we refer to as reality.

First, we view all sentient beings as worthy sages and ourselves as ordinary people. Second, we view all sentient beings as kings and ourselves as commoners. Third, we view all sentient beings as teachers and ourselves as disciples. Fourth, we view all sentient beings as parents and ourselves as children. Fifth, we view all sentient beings as lords and ourselves as servants.

How many people can do that? Christ exemplified this when he washed his disciples' feet. Here, Bodhidharma is giving the same teaching: Serve all beings.

Bodhidharma continued: *The six paramitas are also called the six deliverances. They are giving, discipline, patience, energetic progress, meditative concentration, and wisdom. These are used to deal with the six planes of existence. When the six senses are pure, the six planes of existence are not born. The six planes of existence are essentially life. If you have no attachments to inner or outer and you spontaneously give, this is* dana paramita, *the perfection of giving. When good and evil are equal and neither can be found, this is* shila paramita, *the precepts. When objects and knowledge are in harmony and no longer at odds, this is the perfection of* kshanti paramita, *patience. When great stillness never stirs as the myriad practices are spontaneously so, this is the perfection of* virya paramita, *energetic progress or right effort. When the wondrous stillness flourishes and the body of reality appears, this is* dhyana paramita, *perfection of meditation. When the wondrous stillness opens into illumination, changeless, eternally abiding, not attaching to anything, this is* prajna paramita, *the perfection of wisdom.*

The dharma gates we commit to master in the third vow can be looked at from many perspectives. We can talk about them in terms of Bodhidharma's teachings. We can present them in terms of how the sixth ancestor expressed it. We can appreciate them in terms of the Eightfold Path, the first revolving of the dharma wheel by the Buddha. The eight gates of practice, correlated to the Eightfold Path, are the way we use the dharma gates as the training matrix at Zen Mountain Monastery.

Right concentration of the Eightfold Path is zazen, the still point from which all activity emerges, and also all activity itself. Zazen is not just sitting cross-legged on the pillow but the manifestation of our very life itself.

Right thought, or right mind, is the face-to-face teaching. The teacher-student relationship is about transmission of the Buddha-mind. But the Buddha-mind is the mind of all sentient beings, and the mind of all sentient beings is Buddha-mind—right from the very beginning. It cannot be given, it cannot be received. Why? Because it is already there. It simply has to be realized. That is what the skillful means of the face-to-face teaching are all about—realizing that Buddha-mind. To realize the Buddha-mind is right thought.

We take up right understanding as academic study—the sutras, Buddhist philosophy, and the psychology that emerges from the teachings.

Right speech, or right expression, is liturgy, making visible the invisible, expressing the common experience of the sangha.

Right action is the precepts, the life of a Buddha manifested in the world. Of all the time in the history of the world, the moral and ethical teachings of the Buddha have never been more desperately needed.

Right effort is body practice. It includes everything from tai chi to washing one's face.

Right mindfulness is art practice, any creative process from the traditional Zen arts to the modern arts. All of these provide a vehicle for taking the teachings and manifesting them in the activity of the world.

Finally, right livelihood is work practice. It encompasses all tasks, from picking weeds mindfully to operating a business and making a profit. There is nothing intrinsically wrong with profit. There is no inherent evil in money. It has to do with how you make it, how you handle it, what you do with it. Right livelihood is a livelihood in which no one is ripped off or destroyed by the process. It should be nourishing, fulfilling, and in harmony with the precepts. It is not so difficult to do, and to do competitively. There are a number of people who are demonstrating that business and dharma can go hand in hand.

All of the dharma gates, whatever their configuration or number, come down to the same truth, the realization of the self. The eighty-four thousand practices and subtle gestures all point to the same place—the nature of the self. Nothing can happen until that much has been realized. All of the frustrations, all of the pain, all of the confusion, all of our multinational and personal conflicts, spring from the same delusion, the separation of self and other. The self is an illusion. It is an idea, a mental construct. It does not exist. When self is finally forgotten, the ten thousand things return to the self, where they have always been. That is, the ten thousand things are realized as the self.

It may appear that in Zen, learning and understanding tend to be pushed aside. This is a misconception and definitely not true in our lineage. The way Master Dogen and other great masters of our lineage understand the verbal teachings, philosophy, and sutras is unique. When Dogen speaks about sutras, he means sutras are the entire universe itself. He said:

There is no space and no time that is not the sutras. They use the words and the letters of absolute truth or employ the language of relative truth. Sometimes they adopt the symbols of heavenly beings or put to use the expression of human beings. The words and the letters of beasts, those of asuras, or those of the hundred grasses and thousands of trees are put into action. For this reason, the long, the short, the square, the round, the blue, the yellow, the red, and the white, marshaling solemnly in the ten quarters of the great universe, are nonetheless the sutras' language and their face. They are the instruments of the Great Way and the scriptures for a Buddhist. When you devote yourself to the study of the sutras, they truly come forth. The sutras in question are the entire universe, mountains and rivers and the great earth, plants and trees. They are the self and others, taking meals, wearing clothes, confusion, and dignity. Following each of them and studying it, you will see an infinite number of unheard-of sutras appear before you—following and studying confusion, following and studying dignity, following and studying the rivers, the mountains, the plants, and the trees.

What does it mean to follow and to study? What does it mean to study the self? How, by studying the self, do we ultimately forget the self? By being intimate. When you are really intimate with yourself, you are intimate with the ten thousand things. When you are intimate with Mu, you are intimate with the ten thousand things. When you are intimate with the breath, with pain, with fear, you are intimate with the ten thousand things, with the whole great universe.

Therefore the sutras, said Dogen, *are the whole body of the Tathagata. To practice the sutras is to realize Tathagata, and to meet the sutras is to greet Tathagata. The sutras are the Tathagata's bones, and hence, the bones are these sutras. If you know the sutras are the bones but do not understand that the bones are the sutras, it is not yet the Way. All things themselves are ultimate reality. Here and now constitutes the sutras. The human world and the heavenly world, the oceans and the empty sky, this world and the other world—all are neither more nor less than the ultimate reality.*

When we sit zazen with the whole body and mind, do the koan with the whole body and mind, chant the sutra with the whole body and mind, practice our art with the whole body and mind, work with the whole body and mind, realize the precepts with the whole body and mind, isn't this the ceaseless practice of thousands of Buddhas, past, present, and future? Isn't this the verification and actualization of the life of the Buddha? This is what vowing to master the dharma gates means. This is a religious vow. It permeates time and space. When we enter into a vow such as this, we enter into the body and mind of the countless Buddhas who have transmitted this incredible dharma from generation to generation down to this time.

These vows, these eight gates, are not reserved for the monastery. This practice is engaged in the world— zazen in the world, study in the world, liturgy in the world, moral and ethical teachings in the world, practicing our body in the world, working in the world. We sometimes forget that. We try to put our spiritual practice into the left pocket and our secular life into the right pocket. But our practice is not an activity that takes place in the world; it is the activity of the world. It is the world itself, functioning, creating, laughing, dancing, crying, loving.

These four vows are our life. These eight gates are our practice. Practice the eight gates and verify your life, which is none other than the body and mind, the life of the Tathagata.

The Fourth Vow

The Buddha Way is unattainable; I vow to attain it. *Butsu do mu jo sei gan jo.*

In reference to the fourth vow, Hui-neng said:

> As to the vow *"We vow to attain supreme*

Buddhahood," when we are able to direct our mind to follow the true dharma on all occasions, and when wisdom always rises in our mind so that we can hold aloof from enlightenment as well as ignorance and do away with truth as well as falsehood, then we may consider ourselves as having realized the Buddha-nature or, in other words, as having attained Buddhahood.

He is speaking here of the dualities. When the dualities, and the separation they imply, cease to be, we encounter intimacy—realization of the Way.

The "Faith Mind Poem" says:

The Great Way is not difficult for those who have no preferences.
When love and hate are both absent, everything becomes clear and undisguised.
Make the smallest distinction, however, and heaven and earth are set infinitely apart.

It is in that discrimination that heaven and earth are separated. The characters used in the fourth vow are *Butsu do mu jo sei gan jo. Butsu do* is "the Buddha Way." The term *Way* has profound significance in Chinese history. It is the central tenet of Taoism. When Buddhism arrived in China, the philosophical Indian terms such as *bodhi, nirvana, prajna, shunyata,* all very metaphysical in their nature, were difficult for the Chinese to translate accurately. The Chinese language was much more practical and there was little room in it to accommodate the loftiness of Indian metaphysics. The process of translation in many instances turned into a process of condensation. *Tao* became the Chinese equivalent for *bodhi* and *prajna.* With time it developed into a key Zen term. *Tao* means "the truth of Zen." *Tao,* in Chinese, refers to a way or a passage where people can come and go. It is also used to indicate the right path for a person to follow. It refers to a moral code of conduct and, more broadly, to the fundamental principle and reality of the universe. The Taoist overtones of the word became part of the Zen tradition. This type of merging occurred elsewhere. Many of the early Zen monasteries were originally Taoist monasteries, and many Zen monks were ordained first as Taoist monks.

In Japan *Tao* became *do,* a word that was used in many of the arts, as in *budo,* the way of the warrior, or *chado,* the way of tea. The arts are referred to as "ways" because their practice is intended to refine our spirituality. But refining spirituality notwithstanding, the original meaning of *Tao,* as it is understood in the dharma sense, is the all-pervading reality that is this very life itself.

There is a dialogue between Nan-ch'üan and Chao-chou about the nature of Tao. Chao-chou, a young monk, about eighteen years old, asked Nan-ch'üan, "What is the Way?" Nan-ch'üan said, "Ordinary mind is the Way." Chao-chou continued, "Then should we direct ourselves toward it or not?" Obviously, he had not heard the first response, "Ordinary mind is the Way." So Nan-ch'üan, with great grandmotherly kindness, again revealed his guts to Chao-chou, "If you move toward it, you go away from it." If the Way is where you already are, any action toward it is an action toward an illusion, an idea, something other than this moment. Chao-chou persisted, "Well, if I don't try, how will I know that it's the true Tao?" Nan-ch'üan said, "The Way doesn't belong to knowing or not knowing. Knowing is an illusion; not knowing is blank consciousness. If you really attain to the Tao of no doubt, it's like a great void, so vast and boundless. How then can there be a right and wrong in the Tao?" At those words, Chao-chou had his first enlightenment experience.

When you hear a reference to the Tao, it is addressing the reality that is not divided by any of the dualities. The "ordinary mind" is beyond dualities. The third ancestor talked about this, line after line, throughout the whole "Faith Mind Poem":

> *The Way is perfect, like vast space where nothing is*
> *lacking and nothing is in excess.*
> *Indeed, it is due to our choosing to accept or reject that*
> *we do not see the true nature of things.*
> *Live neither in the entanglements of outer things nor in*
> *the inner feelings of emptiness.*
> *Be serene in the oneness of things.*

And again he said:

> *Do not remain in the dualistic state.*
> *Avoid such pursuits carefully.*
> *If there is even a trace of this and that, right and*
> *wrong, mind essence will be lost in confusion.*

And,

> *When no discriminating thoughts arise, the old mind*
> *ceases to exist.*
> *When the thought-objects vanish, thinking subject*
> *vanishes.*

This is the same thing that the sixth ancestor was saying when he stated, "When it's realized, we can hold aloof from enlightenment as well as ignorance and do away with truth as well as falsehood." That is going beyond the same dualities. If ordinary mind is the way, it reaches everywhere.

The special quality of all these vows is their impossibility. The Buddha Way is unsurpassable; I vow to attain it. It cannot be attained. Even the Buddhas have not attained it. The blue-eyed barbarian Bodhidharma has not attained it. Why can it not be attained? Because we already have it. It cannot be given; it cannot be received.

Butsu do is the Buddha Way. *Mu* means "no" or "nothing." *Mu jo* means "nothing above," "having no top." The Buddha Way is unsurpassed, peerless, unexcelled. I have difficulty with these translations because the implication is that Buddhism is the only way to realization; if you are practicing any other form of religion, it is fruitless. That is not the intention of the teachings of Buddhism. A more accurate translation is "boundless" or "unattainable." "No top," "peerless," or "unsurpassable" suggests a hierarchical sense of the Way. The clearer sense of it is as all-encompassing: it does not exclude anything. Heaven and hell are included, good and bad are included, this religion and that religion are also included, self and other are included. There is nothing that is not included. It reaches everywhere. That is the definition of the Way, and that is the realization of those who have "attained" the Way. That is what the Way is.

Sei gan again stands for "prayerful vow." And the final word, *jo,* "to become," "turn into," "to consist of," "to accomplish," "to attain," "to complete," "to perfect." Any of these words fits. I like "attain" because of the clear tension it creates—"attaining the unattainable," attaining that which we already are.

To make something real is to experience it with the whole body and mind. That is what this whole dharma is about. When that happens, it is our life. It is kind of funny that it is our life whether we realize it or not. All these Buddhas are running around, perfect and complete, lacking nothing, without realizing it. Odd, isn't it?

In a sense, each of these four vows is saying the same thing: no separation. How do you save all sentient beings? No separation. How do you put an end to desires? No separation. How do you master the dharma? Be it. How do you realize the Way? Be the Way.

In *Fukanzazengi*, Dogen began by saying, "The Way is basically perfect and all-pervading. It reaches everywhere. So how could it be contingent on practice and realization? The dharma vehicle is free and untrammeled. The whole body and mind is far beyond the world's dust." Further on he said, "And yet, if there's the slightest discrepancy, the Way is as distant as heaven from earth." The instant the dualities pop up, we lose the Way. Then he goes on to speak of zazen—the heart of practice. The four vows collapse into zazen. That is what that "Be it!" is all about. Dogen said, "The zazen that I speak of is not learning meditation. It is simply the dharma gate of repose and bliss, the practice-realization of totally culminated enlightenment. It is the manifestation of ultimate reality. You will no longer be trapped as in a basket or a cage."

It is that cage that keeps these vows from being realized. We put ourselves inside the cage and put the truth outside. "Once its heart is grasped," Dogen said, "you're like the dragon when it enters the water, like the tiger when it enters the mountain. For you must know that just there, in zazen, the right dharma is manifesting itself and that from the very first, dullness and distraction are struck aside." The cage cannot survive that vast heart of the Way.

The sixth ancestor said the same thing:

Bodhidharma says the great path is fused with mind, revealing the true pattern of reality. All the worthy sages, past and future, have entered through this gate. For those who awaken, the triple world is only mind. Those who do not awaken create dreams as they sleep. The school of the Mahayana must deal with forms and reveal the real. Those who are completely awake know that all phenomena are peaceful and still, and that causal connections produce events, and that temporary combinations give rise to names. Those who do not comprehend become attached to names and abide in words, grasp concepts and run around misguided. When your contemplation has power, you are still not beyond this meaning. Mindfulness reaches the other shore, and you are constantly in the deepest meditative concentration. If you practice this for a long time without stopping, naturally everything will be accomplished.

When we use the term *zazen*, we mean the eight gates of our practice. We do not only mean sitting cross-legged on the cushion but also the face-to-face teaching, the study of the sutras, the liturgy, and the precepts; body practice, art practice, work practice. By *zazen* we mean this very life itself.

"The Buddha Way is unattainable; I vow to attain it." Some may attain it and some may not. Whether we attain it or not, the bottom line is just this: This very body is the body of the Way. This very life is the life of the Buddha.

CHAPTER 15

Jukai:
Opening Our Eyes

When the true eye opens, everything becomes one. When the dharma eye opens, one becomes everything. When the true eye functions, it sweeps all discriminating thoughts away and allows us to see the quality of the Dharmakaya, the absolute oneness of all things. When the dharma eye functions, it eliminates all separation and allows us to realize that nothing is hidden in the universe. Everything is just as it is. The true eye is the eye of wisdom, which, like the diamond sword of Manjushri, cuts off all illusions and delusions. The dharma eye is the eye of compassion, whose unconditioned love, boundless as the mercy of Samantabhadra Bodhisattva, rescues all beings from suffering.

— Maezumi Roshi

Everybody, all beings, have the two eyes, as does the Buddha. When we open both eyes, we see the Buddha-mind. When we see the Buddha-mind, we realize that self-nature and Buddha-nature are not two but one. To realize this is to realize the heart of the precepts, the heart of being.

These precepts are not a culmination of training but rather a beginning, the beginning of a moral and ethical journey in a world that seems to be almost devoid of moral fiber. It is a difficult journey, no question about it. Receiving these precepts is in a sense a challenge to any of us, to realize them and actualize them in everything we do. In giving and receiving these precepts, teacher and student form a bond, a spiritual bond that transcends time and space. It is a bond not only with each other but also with all Buddhas and ancestors that have preceded us and will follow us. Indeed, it verifies and actualizes the life of all Buddhas, past, present, and future. To give and receive the precepts is a very personal matter. I take it personally and I hope you do. Institutions cannot give and receive the precepts. Only people can—Buddhas—from Buddha to Buddha. Please practice them well. Nourish yourself and others. Give life to the Buddha.

PART II

*Koans on Moral
and Ethical Teachings*

CHAPTER 16

Sexuality:
Practicing the Red Thread

The topic of Buddhism and sexuality has become especially relevant in the course of Buddhism's making the transition to a distinctly Western style of practice. For the first time in the history of this religion, men and women are living and practicing together. Students have struggled to practice together in spiritual communities while still functioning in a society that communicates very confused messages about sexual ethics. Teachers' sexual transgressions with their students have been well documented, and though attempts have been made by individual centers to establish guidelines for how teachers should behave and how problems should best be handled, there remains a great deal of misunderstanding and disillusionment about sexuality. Though in recent years more attention has been given to questions revolving around human passions in the context of Buddhist practice, confusion still reigns. In this koan of Master Sung-yuan's "The Red Thread of Passion," I want to explore the nature of passions and their function in practice.

The prologue points to the key issue addressed by the koan:

Intimate and in harmony with the whole reality, it is realized right then and there. In accord with the flow of things, one is able to turn things around and assume responsibility directly. As soon as there is affirmation and denial, the mind is lost in the sea of "yes" and "no." To act freely and unrestrainedly, just as one wishes, is the self-styled practice of anything-goes Zen. To sit blankly, in quietism, is the practice of a corpse. To proceed is to miss the teachings. To retreat is to deny the truth. To neither proceed nor retreat is a dead person breathing. So tell me, what will you do?

The first line, "Intimate and in harmony with the whole reality," is basically a statement of nonseparation. Dogen said, "Seeing form with the whole body and mind, hearing sound with the whole body and mind, one understands them intimately." This intimacy is enlightenment itself.

"In accord with the flow of things, one is able to turn things around and assume responsibility directly." This is the other side. One side is the absolute, the other side is the relative. One is realizing the nature of the self, the nature of reality; the other is the actualizing of that realization in the world, being in accord with the flow of things, being master of one's own life and destiny. When we realize the ground of being, we take responsibility directly, because what we realize is that what we do and what happens to us are the same thing. There is no one to blame. Cause and effect are one. When we realize that fact, responsibility is a natural consequence. When we take responsibility for our anger, for instance, we empower ourselves to do something about anger. As long as we believe that anger is the result of someone else's actions, there is nothing we can do about it. We are victims.

The responsibility that emerges with realization is not limited to what is happening to us. It embraces the whole catastrophe. It includes everything everywhere, throughout time and space—past, present, and future. There is no separation. "As soon as there is affirmation and denial, the mind is lost in the sea of 'yes' and 'no.'" "Yes" and "no" are representative of all the dualities: self and other, this and that, absolute and relative, male and female, up and down, good and bad.

There are also the dualistic extremes of practice. "To act freely and unrestrainedly, just as one wishes, is the self-styled practice of anything-goes Zen." This is *buji* Zen—the "I do whatever I want" approach to life. But that is not freedom. The freedom of license is not real freedom. It is just another hook. On the other hand, "To sit blankly, in quietism, is the practice of a corpse." Letting go of everything, cutting off all ties, sitting on top of some mountain peak, is not what our life is about. It is about being in the world. If our practice does not function in the world, what is the point of it? Our insight has to manifest in everything we do, particularly in terms of human relationships. "To proceed is to miss the teaching. To retreat is to deny the truth." Here again are two opposing poles. The basic question remains of how to transcend the dualities. "To neither proceed nor retreat is a dead person breathing." That takes care of that! Now, what do we do? How do we live our lives? How do we practice?

In the main case of the koan, an ancient teacher points to a problem as old as humanity itself:

*Master Sung-yuan, addressing the assembly, said,
"In order to know the Way in perfect clarity, there is one
essential point you must penetrate and not avoid: the red
thread of passion that cannot be severed. Few face the
problem, and it is not at all easy to settle. Attack it
directly without hesitation, for how else can liberation
come?*

The "red thread of passion" is an expression used in
Zen to describe the deep emotions that all human beings
experience and deal with. Shakyamuni Buddha had to
deal with them. All the ancestors had to deal with them.
The dictionary defines passion as "intense feelings, such
as grief, rage, love, or eager desire." When passion settles
in our genitals we call it lust.

In Zen writings, when there is reference to sexuality
it is usually used to point to the condition of being in the
world. It is a statement of everyday reality just like "rice
in the pail, water in the bucket" and "the valley spirit."
The practice of the Mahayana, and particularly of Zen,
does not end with realization, the peak of the mountain.
It does not end with the falling away of body and mind.
The path continues from the peak, down the other side,
back into the marketplace, back into the world, where
that realization is actualized, manifested in everything
that we do. It never ends.

With regard to the experience of sexuality and physical love, what is the middle way between extreme avoid-
ance and extreme indulgence? The history of Buddhism
presents us with examples of both of these misguided attitudes. On the one hand, there were people who in order
to deny or avoid their sexuality castrated themselves or
scarred themselves so they would not be attractive. On
the other hand, there were those in history who decided
the more sexual activity they engaged in, the freer they

were. It was orgiastic abandonment under the guise of personal freedom. But what is the right way?

Conditioning is a fascinating and subtle phenomenon. What we sometimes call freedom or liberty can be just another way of tying ourselves up. The idea of freedom is like a tether that allows us to go only so far. And, most significantly, it is a self-created tether. Nobody puts it around your neck but you, and you are the only one who can take it off. It limits how far you can go. It creates the boundaries that define your life. It is all part of conditioning.

I once had a dog who was trained not to go into the living room. He could go into any other room in the house. He behaved as if there were an invisible wall at the entrance to the living room. He just wouldn't go in. When my friends got the dog playing retrieving a ball, they would occasionally throw the ball into the living room. The dog would run full speed to the door's threshold, and then he would stop as if he hit a wall. Our conditioning presents us with very similar walls into which we are continuously bumping—nonexistent walls that have the power to stop us dead in our tracks, over and over again.

There are abundant stories about the freewheeling and unrestricted behavior of ancient masters. There have even been books written about the iconoclasm of Zen teachers. People consistently misunderstand these stories and try to imitate these teachers without really appreciating the basic truth of the teachings. The teachings cannot be taken out of context. The specifics of the historical time, cultural patterns, teacher's style, and student's accomplishments and barriers have to be appreciated. We need to understand the time, the place, the position, and the degree characterizing each interaction. That is the way the precepts work. That is the way moral decisions are made.

The teachings did not happen in a vacuum. You cannot simply transplant them from one century to another, from one continent to another. It does not work that way. The essential principles of Buddhism are the same, but the skillful means in which they manifest are in perpetual flux, adapting to circumstances as they are encountered. The student points to the relative, the teacher points to the absolute. The student points to the absolute, the teacher points to the relative. The student points to neither side, the teacher manifests the sixteen-foot golden body of the Buddha.

Shakyamuni taught in India according to the circumstances of that time and society, taking into account the wealth of yogic techniques and the vast metaphysical structure of Hinduism. The early Chinese teachers freely borrowed from Taoist tradition, respecting the practical, down-to-earth attitude of the native students. When Dogen taught in Japan in the thirteenth century, he was dealing with particular problems unique to that period. Monastic schedules were filled with elaborate and esoteric services, complex ceremonies, an aggrandizement of the sacred. The central point of liturgy was missed. Dogen stated that true liturgy had to do with how we clean our teeth, how we use a lavatory, how we wash our face and prepare a meal. In his collection of talks in the *Shobogenzo,* he emphatically stresses that golden robes and endless chanting had nothing to do with liturgy. He dismantled a structure that people had invested with meaning and become attached to.

At one ancient monastery, students were attached to Buddha images, so their teacher burned the statues on the altars. In America, right from the outset of Buddhist practice, Americans wanted to burn Buddha images in the spirit of independence and self-reliance. It was supposed to be an expression of freedom. It is quite clear to me that what we need in this society is to learn how to bow to Buddha images, not burn them. We need to learn how to serve and how to express gratitude.

What was acceptable at one time is not acceptable at another time. A taboo in one area of the world is the norm in another. People change; teachings change. That is why the precepts are not fixed. That is why when you really understand the precepts, you understand how dynamic they are and how they are the manifestation of the Five Ranks of Tung-shan, the interpenetration of relative and absolute. There are no generalities that can be made. There is no fixed set of rules to define anything. Each person needs to go very deep into himself or herself to find the foundation of this practice. You are not going to get it served on a silver platter. Buddhism does not have the answers to our questions—only we do.

What are the passions of grief, rage, love, and sex? When we carefully study an emotion such as anger, we will find that it is directly associated with thoughts. There is a sequence of thoughts that emerge out of one specific thought, which leads to a chain reaction. An event triggers a reaction. The first thought leads to the next thought, and the next thought, and the process rapidly accelerates. Depending on a person's predispositions, at a certain point this process reaches a critical intensity where it shifts from a mental sequence into a full-blown physiological response. Your eyes roll back into your head, you see red, drool is running out of the corner of your mouth, your fists are clenched, and you want to kill. All that began with a thought. If you can clearly and with equanimity experience the first thought, or better yet, the source of the first thought, you can deal with anger. Once the chain reaction gets going, it is difficult, if not impossible, to modify it or stop it.

Focusing on the individual lines of the main case of the koan, I will try to clarify some of the points, keeping in mind that the paramount issue or question addressed by the koan is our relationship with our passions. The first line says, "Master Sung-yuan, addressing the assembly, said . . ." He's gone astray even before he opened his mouth. There is a big difference between the words and ideas that describe reality and reality itself. In addressing the students, every teacher raises the incredible stink of Zen and misses the point, because words always do miss it. We call the activity of teaching "wallowing in mud, gouging healthy flesh and making wounds."

The next line: "In order to know the Way . . ." What way is he talking about? Where is it? What is it? Sitting in a pile of manure, he is searching for the smell! It reaches everywhere. It is not something that you know. In knowing, there is always the separation between the knower and the thing the knower knows. "In order to know the Way in perfect clarity." Knowing has always been dull—never clear. There is no such thing as perfect clarity and knowing. Then Master Sung-yuan said, "There is one essential point you must penetrate and not avoid: the red thread of passion . . ." This is easy to say and hard to do. It is a question that virtually everybody faces in one way or another. Lay practitioners and monastics all struggle with it. It is a major theme of most marriages and relationships.

Human sexuality is at once a great gift and a great hindrance. I remember the endless hours in my mid-twenties spent amid all-pervading sexual fantasies. I used to hate it because I could not get them out of my head.

When I wanted to do my work, they would repeatedly come up; the more exciting the work, the more exciting the fantasies.

Like any other important quality or aspect of our nature, sexuality is not something that can be suppressed or denied. There are appropriate ways of dealing with it but, again, there are no generalities. People are different. For one person, a celibate practice is a practice of ease. For another, it is an excruciatingly frustrating path. Many people love zazen. Others sit out of pure, raw discipline, just enduring. If my relationship to zazen had been like that, I would not have lasted two hours, let alone twenty years. If you do not love it, how can you really do it? This practice should not be a matter of forcing yourself to do something that is not arising out of your heart. There are different practices for different people. Buddhism offers many styles. It is not an accident. They evolved because of various students' inclinations and levels of understanding.

Taking into account our predispositions, tendencies, and personalities, and the fact that passions are universal, how do we practice the Middle Way, avoiding artificial and destructive extremes? One way is to practice the precepts. The precepts essentially point to the path that is walked by a Buddha. The third grave precept says: Honor the body; do not misuse sexuality. This means not being self-centered in sexuality; not using sexuality to manipulate or exercise power. It means being loving in sexuality. It does not mean abandoning sex, unless the person has taken a vow of celibacy. It involves practicing not self-centered sex, not-two sex.

People think that when we talk about nonattachment, we are talking about not loving. Nonattachment is nonattachment. It is not not loving. It is not attaching to love. In fact, there cannot be loving until there is nonattachment. In order to attach you need two entities, which signifies separation. When the gap between the two has disappeared, there is only one reality. That is love. Not Hallmark greeting cards love, not Hollywood Paramount Pictures love, but flesh-and-blood love.

The next line in the koan reads, "Few face the problem . . ." Denial is one of the usual ways in which we avoid our problems. We sidestep them. Our personal and collective histories are filled with instances of denial. When you look through the literature of Zen, you will not find much writing on sex. Everybody's hormones are stirring but nobody talks about it. We have to talk about it. If we are not talking about it, we are evading an important issue, one that always becomes clearer and less likely to create problems if aired out and brought to the light of day. Our practice is not a practice of evasion but a practice of intimacy.

The next line says, "It is not at all easy to settle." Not difficult, not easy. Not either of those two polarities. Where do they come together? "Attack it directly without hesitation or retreat." Attack what? Retreat to where? From what? Who will do it? There is no place to run. No one to do the running. When you realize that, the problem is solved. The last line says, "For how else can liberation come?" Liberation is already the life of each one of us. It is something to be realized, not to be acquired. It doesn't come from anywhere. Nobody is going to give it to you. No one can receive it. You are the only one who can make it happen. And you do that by going deep into yourself to find the foundations of your life.

There are some people who are able to practice celibacy. There are also centers around the country that supposedly have monastics who are celibate, but when we look carefully, we find it is celibacy in name only. They are not celibate. But there is a real practice of celibacy. Just like true zazen, it is not about suppression or denial or gutting it out. It has to do with transmutation of sexual energy. Energy is energy. When you feel it in your heart, it is love. When you feel it in your genitalia, it is sex. You can move it around. When it is on the edge of your fist, it is impact energy. When it is in your legs, it is the ability to run. Our practice allows us to use our energy to benefit all beings. Greed, anger, and ignorance—the three poisons—have another side. When they are turned over, transmuted, they become compassion, wisdom, and enlightenment. We all have the ability and the power to turn things around, to go with the flow, to be free and unhindered in the world.

What this whole catastrophe boils down to is agreement, commitment, and responsibility. That is the glue that holds this world together. That is what makes relationships work. A relationship starts with an agreement. You talk and agree on what the basis of the relationship is. Then, that agreement becomes a commitment. If circumstances change—as they do—you don't just break the commitment. You don't unilaterally go your own way. You return to the discussion, to the agreement, and either you change the agreement to mutual satisfaction or you agree to end the agreement. This is called communication. This applies to any mature relationship: husband-wife, teacher-student, parent-child. They are centered on agreement, commitment, and taking responsibility.

What kind of sexuality is responsible sexuality? It has got to do with caring. It has got to do with not being self-centered. It has got to do with knowing the consequences of your actions. It is about loving and nonattachment. It is not about imitating or accepting others' rules.

The Buddha Way is not about belief systems. It is

not about understanding. It is about empowering yourself, realizing yourself, finding the answers yourself—your own direct experience of realization, and then the actualization of that realization in the world. It is not about Shakyamuni's, Dogen's, or your teacher's realization. It has to flow out of your heart.

The third ancestor said, "When love and hate are both absent, the Way is clear and undisguised." How do we practice neither love nor hate?

> *I love you.*
> *This is loving the self,*
> *loving loving,*
> *being loved by loving,*
> *being loved by the Way.*
> *Isn't this the same as loving a mountain*
> *or a river, a bird or a tree;*
> *loving a person, loving you, loving the self?*
> *My love for you is you;*
> *your love for me is me.*
> *This is true not only for love*
> *but for all activity.*
> *This is true not only for sentient beings*
> *but for the myriad dharmas.*
> *I love you.*

The verse to the koan is a poetic summary of its theme:

> *Since there is neither self nor other,*
> *Where then can there be attacking or retreating?*
> *"Thus I have heard" are the words and ideas*
> *That describe the truth.*
> *What is the truth itself?*

The nature of adamantine wisdom
Is free of even a particle of dust.
The great blue heron comes and goes,
Leaving no traces
And yet it knows how to go its own way.

What is the truth itself? "The nature of adamantine wisdom is free of even a particle of dust." There is nothing foul in it. It reaches everywhere. It encompasses everything, excludes nothing. The great blue heron is like that. It just comes and goes, leaving no traces. It knows precisely what to do and how to go its own way without understanding, without believing, without any trappings.

Buddhism does not have the answers to your questions. I don't have the answers to your questions. History does not have the answers to your questions. You do. *Only* you do. The answer and the question are the same thing. Zen is a process, not an answering machine. It is a process for finding the truth in yourself. To find out, engage it. Go deep into yourself and find that way of using your mind and living your life in peace and in harmony with yourself and the ten thousand things. That red thread of passion cannot be severed. It must be practiced, practiced the same way we practice the precepts, practiced the same way we practice the breath. It is no small thing. It is about this very life itself. The sooner we resolve it, the sooner the struggle is over and the Way is clear and undisguised.

CHAPTER 17

Self-Styled Zen:
T'ou-tzu's All Sounds

Each koan, dharma, experience, or event can be understood on a multiplicity of levels. How much we see depends on our capacity and our clarity. In general, when people are working with koans, it is common that they see the first layer of a koan and want to stop there. They see some part of the koan and think that what they've seen is good enough, at least it is better than nothing. It is easy and quite common to approve oneself, to close the investigation and retreat to the place of certainty. Throughout my twenty-five years of practice, at least once every six months I figured that what I saw was the nature of reality in its completeness. A few steps further along the way I would think that now, at last, this is it; now I've got it! The next year it would repeat itself— this is it; now I've got it!—and the process would go on and on and on.

This practice, this life, is a continuum. It does not

stop at some specific place or time. It is not going to be "finished" somewhere, somehow. The dharmas are boundless. They have no edges. When we collide with the barrier of a koan, an experience, event, or encounter, and we stop and turn away, usually right behind the obstruction there is a gold mine of dharma. It takes effort, tenacity, and lots of patience to take on all the opportunities and exhaust them completely, but the challenges are always there, waiting for us.

In work practice there is a clear difference between an acceptable and an excellent job. Somehow we tend to stop and settle at the first edge—the "it's okay, good enough" zone. For that reason, a lot of Western Zen is still taking place on a very superficial level, at best, and as a self-styled, anything-goes *buji* Zen at its worst. I thought that the "I don't know, I don't care, and it doesn't matter anyway" interpretation of Zen by the Beat generation of the fifties was dead—but it's not. It still reverberates in Zen circles around the country. Recently I heard a teacher expounding the dharma, proclaiming that what Zen was all about was "enjoying the spring, your sexuality, and a glass of good Italian wine." Everybody in the audience chuckled approvingly, loving it. Whatever happened to wisdom, compassion, and the precepts? It is not that the above statement is not true. It is just that it was blatantly out of context and consequently misleading.

It is the same confused understanding and lack of grounding in personal practice and realization that leads both dilettantes and scholars of Zen to make statements that Zen is amoral and beyond morality. D. T. Suzuki said it. Alan Watts said it. Although they made it sound right, both were implicitly dead wrong. Zen is not amoral. It is a practice that takes place within a very definite, clear context that is most definitely moral and ethical.

In *The Blue Cliff Record* collection of koans, there is a koan, "T'ou-tzu's All Sounds," that illuminates these issues. It points out how easy it is to become confused and misinterpret the teachings in a self-serving way. In the pointer, one translation has Master Yüan-wu exclaim, "The Great Way manifests itself naturally. It is bound by no fixed rules." So, isn't that saying that everything I do and am is practice? Isn't that Zen? In that scheme of things a shout, pounding the table with the stick, cooing "Hey, baby, this is your Big Papa," are all dharma. Well, sorry, not good enough. Not on this mountain, not at this training center. Manjushri lives at this monastery, and Manjushri is about wisdom. Kannon Bodhisattva lives here, and she is the very manifestation of compassion. She is about intimacy and giving yourself completely for the sake of all beings. Here you cannot get away with anything-goes Zen. It just does not reach it and it will not work.

It seems that in the West we try to adjust Zen teachings to fit our personal and cultural notions and expectations. Frequently the teachings are altered to satisfy the spiritual customer. In one of the Buddhist journals, somebody recently wrote an article about morality and Buddhism, saying that there are many teachers in this country who abuse power, mishandle money, and sexually harass their students. In the next issue of the magazine, a practitioner responded with a letter eloquently defending this questionable behavior as a form of tantric teachings. He used himself as an example and described how he was seduced by his teacher, and how he learned and benefited in the process. This prompted a further barrage of letters, debating his story and sentiments. And it will go on and on and on—letters, discussion, opinions. Can we really get to the heart of this incredible dharma with debate? Arguments and discussions work well when you operate within a reference system. Debate has a specific function in the Judeo-Christian framework. Rabbis and Jesuits are great debaters. Even in some Buddhist lineages there is attention paid to the cultivation of debating skills. But the dharma of nonduality, the exquisite teaching of formless form, can only be realized directly.

In the pointer of this koan, Master Yüan-wu began, "When this great function manifests before you, it doesn't keep to patterns and rules." What is the great function, and how does it manifest? Where can it be found? Do you think it is you? Well, it is not you. Only when you realize that it is not you does it function. And then there are no patterns and rules, because there are no edges. We bring our reference system into practice and try to practice on the basis of it. This simply does not work. We come into practice because of dissatisfaction with our reference system and then, promptly, we recreate it. We bring all our neurotic behavior into practice and wonder why practice does not work. We have not yet seen the difference between neurotic practice and practicing one's neurosis. And there is a big difference.

In the midst of neurotic practice, we end up justifying our violations of the precepts, confusing greed, anger, and ignorance with enlightenment. How does the practice get sidetracked like that? The main case of this koan takes up this question:

A monastic asked T'ou-tzu, "All sounds are the sounds of the Buddha—right or wrong?" T'ou-tzu said, "Right." The monastic said, "Teacher, doesn't your asshole make farting sounds?" T'ou-tzu hit him. Again the monastic asked, "Coarse words or subtle talk all return to the primary meaning—right or wrong?" T'ou-tzu again said, "Right." The monastic said, "Can I call you an ass, Teacher?" T'ou-tzu then hit him.

What the monastic was quoting was quite correct. The trees, birds, mountains, and streams all recite the name of the Buddha, honor the Dharma, harmonize with the Sangha. The Flower Garland Sutra says it. The national teacher confirmed it. Tung-shan was enlightened by the koan on the teachings of the insentient. So, isn't it true? What is the difference between the sounds of the wind in the pine trees and a fart? What was T'ou-tzu's hit about? Why did he hit the monastic? Was he saying, "That's not it. This is it!" Or was he saying, "Wrong!" Or was he saying, "Go deeper and see it." Or was he expressing approval with the hit?

Yüan-wu says that this monastic had "taken his views of sound and form and stuck them to his forehead." Whenever he met someone, he would immediately ask his questions. But T'ou-tzu was an adept. He was able to discern the oncoming winds. What does it mean to wear your views on your forehead? That is the place where we can easily go wrong with our practice. It is much more difficult to practice today than it was ten, twenty, or thirty years ago. It is getting more difficult because we are getting more sophisticated and familiar with the jargon of Buddhism. We get lost in the words, thinking that if we can define or explain something, we are intimate with it.

Twenty years back there were hardly any reliable translations of koans. At the Zen Center of Los Angeles we used mimeographed copies of the typed-out main case. That was it. There were no further references, comparative translations, bibliographies. We just kept coming back to that central question "What is it?" Today we are inundated with texts, essays, taped *teishos*. There are stockpiles of dharma talks. Hungry, we listen and read and grab onto the words and ideas, making a nest there.

Sometimes we take it further—we paste the "truth" on our foreheads and prance around converting others. We expound the dharma of the head instead of what arises in our hearts.

The monastic in this case had some understanding—no question about it—but it was all up in his head. It had not yet encompassed the whole body and mind. Feeling confident, he figured that he would test the old master. The lines were his standard fare, wherever he visited. Absorbed in his view, he did not see that T'ou-tzu was fishing. With each response the teacher put bait on the hook. The monastic climbed onto it, and T'ou-tzu reeled him in. It is interesting and unfortunate that despite T'ou-tzu's effort the monastic still did not get it. People who are this thick stick for years in the same rut. It is very difficult to see the blind spots of our egos.

In the commentary Yüan-wu says, "He just sees that the awl point is sharp. He doesn't see that the chisel edge is square." The monastic is seeing only one side of reality, one aspect of it. "Though he has waves that go against the current, yet he has no horns on his head." He can make waves. He can challenge the teacher and pull the tiger's whiskers. It is easy to do that, especially in this country and culture where entitlement and confrontation are our familiar refrains. It does not take any intelligence. But it takes courage and wisdom to really hear the teachings.

When the monastic said, "Coarse words or subtle talk all return to the primary meaning," T'ou-tzu replied, "Right." Just like the first answer—exactly and precisely correct. There is no difference. The monastic then said, "Can I call you an ass, Teacher?" T'ou-tzu hit him. The key here is to appreciate what was going on with T'ou-tzu. Again, what was that hit? What was the teaching? Was T'ou-tzu disapproving? Was the monastic wrong? If he was wrong, why did T'ou-tzu say he was right? If he was right, why did T'ou-tzu hit him? Is there a difference between the sound of the wind in the pine trees and the sound of a fart? Is one the Buddha's voice and the other not? It is not such a wild and far-fetched question. People ask me, "Why do I have to take off my rakusu when I go to the bathroom?" They don't understand. The rakusu seems ordinary. Is it something holy? Is the monastic robe different from dungarees? When somebody is asking such questions the seeds of *buji* Zen are already sprouting.

Hsüeh-tou began his poem on this koan with the following line: "T'ou-tzu, T'ou-tzu, the wheel of his ability is unobstructed. He releases one and gets two." Is he being arbitrary? We see such apparent arbitrariness in koans. One master says one thing, another master contradicts him. A monastic asked, "Does a dog have Buddha-nature?" Chao-chou said, "No." Another monastic came. "Does a dog have Buddha-nature?" Chao-chou said, "Yes." Anything goes, right? Say whatever you want and that is the dharma. When in doubt, shout or jump around a little bit. Isn't Zen about being free and crazy?

The verse continues: "How pitiful—innumerable people playing in the tide, in the end fall into the tide and die." This is a reference to playing in the riptide. There is an actual place in China, with a beautiful but dangerous beach, famous for its surf, particularly in the summer and autumn. Lots of people come and play in it. And very often the reckless ones lose their lives. The tide carries them into the ocean and they drown because they are unable to get back to the beach. Hsüeh-tou comments that thousands of Zen practitioners world over are playing in the tide, and in the end they fall into the tide and die.

Yüan-wu adds, "Too bad, but what can they do? They can't get out of the trap." The trap is the nest we've been living in all our lives. We think that we can just package it up and bring it with us and practice within it. That is neurotic practice. To practice that is to practice neurosis. Do you see the difference? Neurotic practice and practicing neurosis is like night and day.

"If they suddenly came to life, the hundred rivers would reverse their flow with a rushing, roaring noise." What is wrong with what that monastic was saying? Is it wrong? If it is not wrong, what is the whole dialogue about and why is it a koan? If it is wrong, what is the teaching that is taking place here? Is he just caught up in the words, or is there something more? It seemed like a reasonable question. After all, it comes from the sutras. It seemed like a reasonable answer from the master. What was all the hitting about?

This dharma cannot be extinguished. I remember receiving a frantic phone call from a Zen student who was also a writer for the *Village Voice*. He called me about someone who was calling himself a Zen master. The writer was very concerned about this man's effect on the Zen community. This self-proclaimed teacher was at the peak of his popularity at the time, packing auditoriums with hundreds of eager listeners. He was very slick and charismatic, and attracted many people who were very impressed with him. But he had no training. He might have had a spontaneous realization, and that is what he was teaching. Many serious Zen practitioners were angry with him and his "success." They had to sit and do sesshins for years, sweating through their barriers and biases, and here this guy becomes a seemingly stellar teacher overnight.

This editor wanted to write a fact-baring exposé. He wanted me to say something against this teacher and was frustrated when I would not do it. He whined, "But he'll destroy the dharma." I said, "How do you destroy the dharma? Would you please explain that to me?" Surprisingly, and slightly reassured, he said, "You know, your dharma brother said exactly the same thing to me." Before reaching me, he had called up Tetsugen Roshi and had a similar conversation with him. It ended with Tetsugen asking, "How do you destroy the dharma?"

This dharma will not be extinguished. It will not be destroyed. It cannot be destroyed. It has always been here. It always will be here, manifesting continually and inexhaustibly. When I say "here," I do not mean this specific place. I mean this great earth, this universe and unimaginable others. The question is, Are you ready to see it and to hear it? All of it, not just the edges or parts that are convenient to access and easy to digest. All of it: the infinitely profound, the minutely subtle, as well as the undeniably obvious.

It is ours if we are willing to have it. But it must be engaged in order to function. That is up to us. We can play in the tide and die, or we can reverse the flow of the hundred rivers. We need to practice with our hearts, not with our minds. Forget the mind. Let the mind fall away. Let the self fall away. See that the great heart of Kannon Bodhisattva is your heart, the heart of all beings. To realize this is the lion's roar of Manjushri. To manifest and actualize this is the compassionate heart of Kannon Bodhisattva. And all of it—all the good stuff and all the bad stuff, all the delusion and the clarity, all that is in harmony with the universe and all that creates pain, suffering, and the barriers of greed, anger, and ignorance—all of it exists within each one of us.

Each one of us is a container of the complete spectrum of human existence, from the most horrifying and repulsive to the most wonderful and attractive. Hitler and

Buddha reside inside each one of us. What we practice is what we manifest. Practice greed and neurosis and you manifest greed and neurosis. Practice wisdom and compassion and you live and breathe wisdom and compassion. We arrived on this earth fully equipped. We have the opportunity to practice this life. We are that opportunity. What will we do?

CHAPTER 18

Cause and Effect:
Pai-chang and the Fox

Among the classical koans that address the moral and ethical issues in our lives, there are few more subtle and insightful than "Pai-chang and the Fox," case 2 from the *Mumonkan: The Gateless Gate* collection. "Pai-chang and the Fox" is a very fine example of a *nanto* koan, *nanto* meaning "difficult to pass through," according to the koan classification of Master Hakuin. The reason it is difficult to pass through is that the key point being made is a very elusive one, very easy to miss or misinterpret. Although this koan appears as the second case, I have students skip over it because of its significance and subtlety, until they have completed all of the other koans in the *Mumonkan*.

Just like the teachings of the precepts, this koan escapes simplistic interpretations or sweeping generalizations, yet it demands clear and precise response. It forces us to look closely at the principle of causality, not as an abstract notion but as the immediacy of each moment and each activity, allowing us to understand more intimately what it means to take responsibility for our lives and the life of this universe.

The main case of the koan tells a story of an encounter between Master Pai-chang and an old man who used to visit Pai-chang's monastery to listen to the master's discourses:

Whenever Master Pai-chang gave teisho on Zen, an old man sat with the monastics to listen and always withdrew when they did. One day, however, he remained behind, and the master asked, "Who are you standing here before me?" The old man replied, "I am not a human being. In the past, in the time of Kashyapa Buddha, I was the head of this monastery. Once a monastic asked me, 'Does an enlightened person also fall into causation or not?' I replied, 'An enlightened person does not.' Because of this I was made to live as a fox for five hundred lives. Now I beg you, please say the turning words on my behalf and release me from the fox body." The old man then asked Pai-chang, "Does an enlightened person also fall into causation or not?" The master said, "An enlightened person does not ignore causation." Hearing this, the old man was at once enlightened. Making a bow to Pai-chang, he said, "I have now been released from the fox body, which will be found behind the mountain. I dare to make a request of the master. Please bury it as you would a deceased monastic."

The master had the ino strike the gavel and announce to the monastics that there would be a funeral for a deceased monastic after the midday meal. The monastics wondered, saying, "We're all in good health. There's no sick monastic in the nirvana hall. What's it all about?" After the meal the master led the monastics to a rock behind the mountain, poked out a dead fox with his staff, and cremated it.

In the evening the master ascended the rostrum in the hall and told the monastics the whole story. Huang-po thereupon asked, "The old man failed to give the correct turning words and was made to live as a fox for five hundred lives, you say. If, however, his answer had not been incorrect each time, what would he have become?" The master said, "Come closer to me, and I'll tell you." Huang-po then stepped forward to Pai-chang and hit him. The master laughed aloud, clapping his hands, and said, "I thought the foreigner had a red beard. Now I see that it is a red-bearded foreigner."

There are many practitioners in this sangha who practice within prison walls. Questions of cause and effect come up frequently in my meetings with them. This is something that many of the prisoners deal with quite passionately. As a consequence of their actions, they have ended up living in a prison. Some of them are in for murder and have been sentenced for life. Many of them, since they began practicing Zen, have come to confront and question the implications of their actions for the first time in their lives.

People tend to protect themselves. We deny, suppress, absorb ourselves in distractions and, in general, avoid the difficult things in our lives. We create a protective coating around ourselves that isolates us from life. When we begin Zen practice, we chip away at that shell. There is a phase when the student becomes very exposed and vulnerable. This is one of the reasons why it is critical for teachers to be responsible, to recognize and work with that vulnerability and not take self-centered advantage of it, as teachers have in the past, not only in our country but in other countries as well. If the openness is used as a way of bringing a student to realization, that is one thing. If it is employed to the advantage of a narcissistically inclined teacher, it is a gross violation of the precepts on the part of that teacher.

Some of the students at the prison who have significantly engaged this practice have become very vulnerable, which can be risky and dangerous, especially behind prison walls. Part of their ability to survive there has to do with their invulnerable posture, the thick shell. The most advanced among them, practicing for eight or more years, have come to grips with causality in their lives, have taken responsibility for it, and have been able to move on. They have come out of that hiding place and begun to manifest clarity in their lives. The practice has actually turned their lives around dramatically enough so that even the prison authorities and the correction officers have recognized the changes that have taken place. Some of the students have been put to work as counselors for other prisoners.

It is one thing to present the great principles of dharma, or to sit and listen to them. It is quite another to confront them honestly with one's own life. That is why koan study, dharma combat, and *mondo* exchanges are so vital to the life and continuity of this practice. They take the teachings out of the theoretical and abstract mode and thrust them into the present moment, giving them immediate, undeniable relevance.

In an attempt to do that at the prison during a Rohatsu sesshin, I presented the students there with a modern version of this koan. A very similar thing happened recently with a dharma teacher here in America who essentially made the statement that his realization, his enlightenment, enabled him to transcend cause and effect. As a result of that assumption, he is presently "living five hundred lives as a fox." So this ancient koan surfaces in the twentieth century, right in our own backyard. People think that koans are archaic historical documents. With any sense of understanding, you will see that they pertain to you and me, each and every day of our lives. They are the continuing process of this life itself.

Instead of asking the prisoners, "What would you have answered if you were Pai-chang?" or "How would you have handled it if you were Huang-po?" or "What would you say to the old man in order to save him from five hundred lives as a fox?"—questions that seem ancient and far away—I reframed the story. I shared with them the specifics of this modern instance of the koan, where a teacher who had contracted HIV had sexual relationships with many of his students, thereby possibly infecting them with the virus. He knew he had the virus, yet he knowingly had relationships without protection and without informing his partners. When asked why he did that, he said that he was convinced that because of his realization he was able to transcend the cause and effect of having AIDS. In other words, his infection would not become an effect for someone else.

The "five hundred lives of a fox" have been the almost complete breakdown of the community of practitioners to whom he was responsible. In the immediate generation, at least one person has been infected, and there may be many more who test positive at a future date. And who knows what the ripple effect of this will be if the infection spreads.

The teacher has now died, suffering all the complications of AIDS. My question to the prisoners was, "What would you do? How would you have handled that situation as the teacher? How would you turn it around?" It was a real dharma combat. People answered from the point of view of where their practice was. One guy said he would throw himself off a cliff, and that is exactly the way he is practicing his life. He is tormented with regret and remorse for having killed many innocent people, not only in this country as a civilian but also as a licensed killer in Vietnam. And that is what we work on. Needless to say, I would not accept his response. I told him it was a cop-out.

How do *you* deal with this koan? It is a good question for all of us to examine deeply. It is one thing to understand the principles of cause and effect, and quite another to see how they function in our lives. None of us is perfect. We are all going to err—no question about it. These are difficult and complicated times. There are no easy solutions. How do we deal with the problems we encounter? What is our understanding of who we are and what the universe is? What is our moral responsibility? How can we practice our lives? What does it mean to be realized? What does it mean when Master Dogen says that practice and realization are one?

In appreciating this koan, the first thing we should look at is the old man. He says, "I am not a human being. In the past, in the time of Kashyapa Buddha, I was the head of this monastery." Kashyapa Buddha is one of the legendary Buddhas who preceded Shakyamuni Buddha. Kashyapa Buddha is the Buddha who supposedly sat for ten thousand *kalpas* under the bodhi tree and never attained enlightenment. So, this old man says that was the time when he was the head of the monastery. At that time a monastic asked him, "Does an enlightened person also fall into causation or not?" Because of his answer he was made to turn into a fox.

What is this old man? What is this fox? To really chew up and digest this koan, you must understand its language. You have to grasp the essence of living the life of a fox. To us, it may seem like no big deal; in fact, it may seem desirable. A fox can look beautiful wandering around the hillsides. For Chinese or Japanese people, however, to be called a fox is the worst thing imaginable. It was a vile curse to call someone a wild fox spirit. The positive associations we have in English to "being foxy"— shrewd, sharp, attractive—just did not apply when this koan appeared. It was derogatory through and through.

For saying that an enlightened person does not fall into causation the old teacher was turned into a fox. Why? The sutras, again and again, say that enlightened beings do not fall into causation. In fact, one of them states, "An errant monastic does not fall into hell. This very place is the absolute place. There is no hell to fall into." It goes on to say, "A holy saint does not go to heaven. This very place is the absolute place. There is no heaven to ascend to." When the whole universe is causation itself, how can there be talk of falling or not falling? In one sense, you can correctly call it "falling" or you can correctly call it "not falling." But if there is even a single thought associated with either of those statements, heaven and earth are separated, and you turn into a fox and fall into hell.

When the old man asked Pai-chang how he would respond, Pai-chang said, "An enlightened person does not ignore causation." How are these two statements—"not falling into causation" and "not ignoring causation"— different? Cause and effect is very clear. It's undeniable. There's nothing on earth that exists outside of the activity of cause and effect. Every moment, every existence, is causation itself. Outside it there is neither self nor other, neither I nor the world. There is no denying it. Master Dogen repeatedly focuses on this point in the *Shobogenzo*. For him, to deny cause and effect is to deny

Buddha-dharma. "Practice is enlightenment" reflects the same relationship. Practice (cause) and enlightenment (effect) are one. Cause and effect are one. This is a basic, quintessential teaching. And if you really understand "Cause and effect are one," you understand that cause does not precede effect, nor does effect follow cause.

Later in the koan Huang-po asks, "If he had answered correctly, what would he have turned into?" I ask you, "What would the correct answer be?" How could that old man have responded to the original question? How could our modern master have practiced his life so as to avoid creating the pain and suffering in his own life and the lives of others? If the old man had answered correctly, what would he have become? Right in that becoming—old man becoming fox, fox turning back into old man—is the clue to the problem that he was dealing with, and the clue to the problem that we all deal with.

When Huang-po challenges Pai-chang with "What would he have turned into if he answered correctly?" Pai-chang says, "Come closer and I'll tell you." That's it! Come a little closer. Huang-po stepped up and hit Pai-chang. What was Huang-po communicating by striking his old teacher? And what was Pai-chang's response all about, clapping his hands and laughing? Was he approving of the hit? When Huang-po struck, was that Huang-po's answer as to what the old man would have become? Pai-chang concludes the exchange with the statement, "I thought the foreigner had a red beard. Now I see that it is a red-bearded foreigner." What is the logic here? What is the communication? What is the old man? What is Pai-chang? What is the fox? None of them are man or fox.

The term *enlightened person* is intended to mean a person who has completed spiritual training, a person of satori who has accomplished emancipation and at last realized peace of mind. Such a person is not subject to retribution or transmigration. The whole point of practice is to free oneself of the chain of causation. That's the whole point of the teachings of Mahayana Buddhism. That is the definition of realization and freedom. It is such an obvious fact among Buddhists that it is not even discussed. It is a given. This is the position presented by the former head of the monastery, the old man, in his reply to "Does an enlightened person also fall into causation or not?" So the question persists—why did he have to live five hundred lives as a fox as a result of his answer? That is a central point of this koan. What does it really mean to be free from cause and effect, from retribution? This is where the truth of this koan, where the truth of Zen, is to be found. "An enlightened person does not fall into causation" will unequivocally turn one into a fox, unless one clearly knows what that truth really is.

Obviously, when he answered the monastic, the old man was uncertain. He became enlightened with Pai-chang's words, but at the time the monastic was questioning him, he was not clear. When he asked Pai-chang, "Now I beg you, please say the turning words on my behalf and release me from the fox body," Pai-chang immediately replied, "An enlightened person does not ignore causation." A turning word is something that is exactly the right statement for a person in a certain state of mind. It is an expression that brings realization. It can actually be anything. Sometimes a shout is a turning word. Sometimes a hit is a turning word. Sometimes just repeating the question becomes the turning word. Turning words are the words that turn one's mind to the truth. In that person's consciousness, it is the ultimate expression of truth.

In a literal way, we can say that Pai-chang's reply means that an enlightened person does not ignore the fact of cause and effect but lives according to it. In a sense, this is diametrically opposed to "Unequivocally, he does not fall into causation." We could also say that what Pai-chang is saying is exactly the opposite of what the Mahayana sutras are saying. It is almost like stating that no matter how enlightened you become, you are still constantly subjected to perpetual rebirth and transmigration. That is a contradiction of the Mahayana definition of enlightenment. Is that Pai-chang's meaning and intention?

Hearing Pai-chang's words, the old man was at once enlightened. That is what the koan tells us. The old man was enlightened when he heard Pai-chang say, "An enlightened person does not ignore causation." If you think for a second that what the old man said, "not falling into causation," is an incorrect reply, and that Pai-chang's answer, "not ignoring causation," is the correct reply, then you're ten thousand miles away from it. Don't fall into that trap. That is what makes this a *nanto* koan. Immediately, we want to get logical. The old man said, "not falling into causation," and he was turned into a fox. Pai-chang said, "not ignoring causation," and he became a person again. Therefore, Pai-chang must be right and the old man must be wrong. Wrong, wrong, wrong, wrong, wrong. That misses it. In fact, another old master said, "Not falling into causation, and he was turned into a fox. The first mistake. Not ignoring causation, and he was released from the fox body. The second mistake." Why does he call them both mistakes? If neither is correct, what is correct?

Also, do not get caught up in the story line. Pai-chang is a very shrewd teacher, and good teachers have a way of concocting complications. I'm sure Pai-chang was out for a walk on the mountain one day and he found a dead fox and said, "Aha!" He took the fox, stuffed it in a cave, and came back to tell the monastics the story about the old man. "Have you noticed the old man who's been coming here?" When you are running a monastery with a thousand monastics, nobody notices if there is a stranger in the back. "Every time there's a *teisho,* he has been here. And after the last *teisho* he told me that he had once been the abbot of this monastery, thousands of years ago, and that he was made to live five hundred lives as a fox simply because when a monastic asked him, 'Does an enlightened being fall into causation or not?' he answered, 'An enlightened person does not,' quoting the sutra. And then he asked me, 'Does an enlightened being fall into causation or not?' and I said to him, 'An enlightened person does not ignore causation.' Immediately, he was freed from the fox body. So come with me and let's bury that dead fox."

All the monastics followed. Behind the mountain, Pai-chang poked out the dead fox, cremated it, and performed a funeral for a monastic. Huang-po, who was Pai-chang's main student, came up and did dharma combat with the old man, making the truth even clearer. He was the only one among the thousand in the assembly who understood the teaching that Pai-chang was putting forth.

To get to another level of appreciation of this koan, we must understand that the fox body is a deluded body. It is that fox body that brings us to practice to begin with. All kinds of different reasons motivate us into practice. For some people it is just a matter of getting answers to questions. Even though these questions may lead us to realization, they usually come from a very deluded point of view. They are essentially life koans. Koans bring us into practice, and koans carry us all the way through practice. It does not matter whether we are doing koan study or sitting *shikantaza,* our questions are our koans. Each time we clarify one, two or three others pop up in its place. Through the process of struggling with them we slowly, deliberately, hone our lives to perfection.

The "fox" that the old man was (and that the modern master I referred to was) represents a deluded point of view. The old man was already a fox before he answered the monastic's question, only he had not realized it. On hearing the words of Pai-chang, he was released from the fox body. Yet, he was always free of the fox body, right from the very beginning, before he became a fox, after he became a fox, and after he returned from being a fox. He was always released from the fox body, only he did not realize it.

That realization is the key. That realization was the basic difference between Pai-chang's statement and the old man's statement. But if you think that the old man was wrong when he said, "An enlightened being does not fall into causation," and that Pai-chang was correct when he said, "An enlightened person does not ignore causation," then you too are speaking from the fox body. Falling into, not falling into; being a fox, not being a fox; being a person, not being a person; correct and incorrect—all are part of the same duality that got this man into trouble in the first place.

"Falling and not falling" is a trap. That's why Dogen teaches that cause and effect are one, not one before and another after. Effect does not follow cause. Cause does not precede effect. They are one moment that totally and completely consumes the whole universe. Realizing Pai-chang's words was the old man's atonement. His atonement was his realization, his at-one-ment. At one with what? At one with the fox body? At one with cause and effect? At one with the old man?

The same thing can be asked regarding the modern master. What is his atonement? That was the question I put to the practitioners at the prison. What would you do to atone? How would you take responsibility for your life in that situation? How would you acknowledge the fact that what you do and what happens to you are the same thing? That is cause and effect. So, what is this modern master's atonement? How can it be realized and actualized? That is the only way to free oneself.

The practice of atonement is the practice of the precepts. When we receive the precepts, we embrace a definition of the life of a Buddha. The precepts are the process that a Buddha uses to actualize life within the world of phenomena. When we practice the precepts, we practice atonement. The realization of atonement, or the realization of the precepts, is enlightenment. It then becomes the manifestation of our life.

If we just accept what the sutras say from an academic perspective, we come to a dead end. We need to make the content of the sutras a vital part of our life; that is what koans do. When I talk about koans, I am talking about everybody's practice. At Zen Mountain Monastery, the people who are doing *shikantaza* also study and work, do art practice, body practice, and liturgy. They don't just sit. It is in all those other aspects of training that *shikantaza* begins to manifest itself. It is toward the *genjo-koans*, the koans of life, that the power of *shikantaza* is directed.

If you just sit, it is very easy to become very passive, placid, and nonfunctional. It is like being dead but not yet buried. With zazen alone, it is all compost but no seeds. Sometimes there are all seeds and no compost. That happens when there is plenty of reading, studying, and intellectualizing but no zazen to nourish it, to allow it to grow, to help it to flower. And what is that flowering? That flowering is the realization of zazen, the actualization of the teachings. The sutras without zazen are just sutras. They are not yet the enlightenment of the Buddha. Liturgy without zazen is just liturgy. It is not yet the manifestation of the teachings of all Buddhas, past, present, and future.

And where does it show up? It shows up in every activity that we do. You can tell who is doing zazen with the whole body and mind. I am not talking about people who are sitting cross-legged, assuming the form of zazen. That is not yet zazen. Let the mind sit along with the body. Unless that is happening, the same old stuff goes on. It can easily become a dharma game.

I was overhearing a number of conversations the other day at a Chinese restaurant in town. There was a table with six people who were evidently Buddhist practitioners. They were involved in an entertaining round of Buddhist gossip. There were three guys sitting next to me talking about the stock market, and across the room there were a couple of people talking about hunting. All the conversations were exactly the same. A waste. I heard the practitioners talking about what the teachers do when nobody is around, telling each other "secrets" the rest of the sangha does not know. It was all words.

That's all nice. That is cocktail Zen. That is *buji* Zen, *buji* Buddhism. That is the Buddhism of the fifties, when people sat around and talked about practice. It is not the flower that blooms out of zazen. It is talking about the flower. That is what this old monastic was doing, talking about cause and effect, quoting the sutra, not having yet realized it. That is what got the modern master in trouble, intellectualizing it, not having realized it. Realization makes all the difference in the world. It directly impacts how you propagate your life and how you relate to other people.

The Vietnamese master Thich Nhat Hanh, addressing a group of people in San Francisco, encouraged them to start a Buddhist community; not a monastery, not a center, but a Buddhist community. They are very common in Asia. He was suggesting that they all practice and let their children practice. He said, "We need people to work in that place. We don't need monastics. We don't need enlightened people. We need happy people, because angry people can't do it. An angry person has nothing to offer a community that's trying to get started. But a happy person, even if stupid, even if deluded, a happy person nourishes, heals, and benefits all those who come in contact with him or her. An angry person poisons, obstructs, and puts out seeds of anger to everyone that comes close. We need happy people."

I agree with him. The problem is that most people are unhappy, and usually what we see as happiness is a facade. It is imitation. Imitation works for a while, but in the long run it falters. We walk around with the big smile, and then when we are alone, the agony appears. That smile does not need to be fabricated. This life is a wonderful gift. It can be lived without difficulty in a way that is in peace and harmony with everything around us. Even if one is condemned to live the life of a fox! When you live the life of a fox through and through, with the whole body and mind, it is a wonderful, happy, and blessed life. It is only when we deny, separate ourselves, move away from, that we create suffering.

In the commentary on the koan, Wu-men says, "Not falling into causation, why was he turned into a fox? Not ignoring causation, why was he released from the fox body? If you have an eye to see through this, then you will know that the former head of the monastery did enjoy his five hundred happy, blessed lives as a fox." This is a wonderful summation of both parts of this koan. First of all, Wu-men is pointing out that the head of the monastery was turned into a fox as a result of his reply. Then he asks, "Why was he released as a result of Pai-chang's answer?"

This becomes a particularly burning question when you realize that his answer was not wrong, nor Pai-chang's answer right. So what is going on? The clue is, "If you have an eye to see through this, then you will know that the former head of the monastery did enjoy his five hundred happy, blessed lives as a fox."

Actually, there is no falling and no releasing. If you can see this from the absolute point of view, what does it really mean to be released from the fox body? What does it really mean to live life as a fox? Wu-men is asking us to throw away all of the complications—turning into a fox, being released from the fox body. Then the way is clear.

Why is it so vital and important to know how to live five hundred happy, blessed lives as a fox? Not to appreciate the pressing nature of that question is to miss the essence of how the koans function in our lives. To know how to live a happy, blessed life as a fox means to be able, under whatever circumstance, to be present with the whole body and mind, through and through. If you're a fox, be a fox with the whole body and mind. There is nothing but fox. There is no longer a reference system. When you cry, just cry, with the whole body and mind. Be crying. Then there is no crying. When you are happy, be happy with the whole body and mind, and then there is no happiness. What does it mean to be "it" with the whole body and mind, to be Mu with the whole body and mind, to be yourself with the whole body and mind? There is no crack in the dharma eye. It is whole, continuous, from the past to the future with no gaps. Seamless.

Wu-men says, "If you have an eye"—that is, the spiritual eye—"to see that fundamentally Buddhas and ignorant beings are one, if you have an eye to see that purity and defilement are one, then you free yourself." The eye he is talking about is the third eye. If you have that eye, the Zen eye of satori, then you will know that the five hundred fox lives were happy and blessed. When the old man is truly an old man, that life is a happy and blessed life. When the fox has transcended falling and releasing and is truly a fox through and through, that life is a happy and blessed life. The happiness goes beyond the five hundred lives. It is eternal happiness, penetrating all places and all ages.

How does one live five hundred blessed lives as a prisoner? How does one live five hundred blessed lives as a world leader? I have seen happy and clear prisoners, and sad, confused, and angry world leaders. So there is obviously more to what peace of mind and joy are about than how much money you have or don't have; than what position, authority, or power you have over others. This does not mean that being meek makes you happy or that being strong makes you happy. It has nothing to do with conditions. It has to do with really knowing yourself—who you are, what your life is—to realize it and to live it out of what you have realized.

In the poem, Wu-men said:

Not falling, not ignoring,
Odd and even are on one die.
Not ignoring, not falling,
Hundreds and thousands of regrets.

Whether we say "not falling" or "not ignoring," all of it, in and of itself, is the essence of truth; not falling with the whole body and mind, not ignoring with the whole body and mind. And yet nothing is ever outside causation. Those relationships always exist—cause and effect, good and bad, enlightenment and delusion—but their elements are not different from each other. Form is exactly emptiness, emptiness exactly form. Cause is exactly effect, effect is exactly cause. It does not make logical sense. Heads is exactly tails, tails is exactly heads. Male is exactly female, female is exactly male. Buddhas are exactly creatures, creatures are exactly Buddhas. Enlightenment is exactly delusion. Delusion is exactly enlightenment. It does not mean that it is a mixture, and it does not mean one or the other. Nor does it mean "Well, if delusion is enlightenment, then I'll do whatever I want. It doesn't matter anyway." That is the result of understanding Zen superficially. It is not form, and it is not emptiness; yet form is exactly emptiness and emptiness exactly form. So where is that place of truth? It is not heads, it is not tails; not one, not two. It is neither one nor two.

The whole problem of the old man, the whole problem of anger, the whole problem of separation, is born of the idea of a self. Attachment is an illusion based on separation. Falling and not falling, form and emptiness, are all based on the illusion of the existence of a self. Attachment to the self is what separates body and mind, what creates fear and anxiety, what creates anger. It also creates attachments to ideas, to words, phrases, slogans, positions, power, authority, and control. It doesn't matter whether we have a big ego or a little ego. An ego trip is an ego trip. "Big-deal self" is an ego trip. "The insignificant self" is an ego trip. "I can't do it" is an even bigger ego trip. "I'm no good. Everyone is better than I am" is the biggest ego trip of all. It's all got to do with self-preservation. There is no self to preserve. What are you holding on to? What are you protecting?

What is the self? What is it that's born? What is it that will die? It all has to do with right now. The past is right now. The future is right now. See what's right here, right now. That is where your life is. That is where your practice is. Buddha is right now. Pai-chang is right now. The old man and the fox are right now. Huang-po is right now.

Wu-men commented, "Whatever it may be, whenever it may be, it is always causation itself. Nothing can ever be outside of causation. Odd and even are on one and the same die. They are, after all, two faces of the same coin. If I say that they are one and the same, people may attach to this oneness and be caught in a net of sameness. Not ignoring or not falling, whatever one may say it is, hundreds and thousands of regrets." And then he asked, "What kind of life is it, this life of hundreds and thousands of regrets?" Then he added that the essence of the entirety of this koan is in the last line—hundreds and thousands of regrets. The key to happy, blessed lives is hidden right there.

Whatever you think this koan means, forget it. It has no meaning whatsoever. If you are looking for meaning, you are wasting your time. This practice has nothing to do with meaning. Meaning is the words and ideas that describe reality. We are not talking about that here. Practice is directly experiencing that reality. That is why we do zazen. Make yourself empty. The only way to see anything is to be it, and the only way to do that is to let go of the self that separates you from it. The only way through a barrier is to be the barrier. The only way that can happen is to forget the self that separates us from the barrier.

That is what the old man at first did not understand but later came to understand. Pai-chang could just as easily have answered, "An enlightened person does not fall into causation." But that's what the old man said, and he became a fox. Would Pai-chang have become a fox, too? Right and wrong is what makes foxes. Good and evil is what makes foxes. Cause and effect is what makes foxes. How is it when there is neither absolute nor relative, cause nor effect, good nor bad, up nor down, fox nor person, teacher nor student, heaven nor hell?

The biggest barrier that most people face is the absolute, unequivocal conviction that they cannot do it, that they will never do it. And they are right. They can't, and they never will—not until they are convinced that they will. You can only go as far as you allow yourself to go. Don't hold back. This life is too precious to waste. Whether we realize it or not, it is boundless. When we do realize it, we free ourselves from that fox body. And not only do we free ourself from that fox body—we simultaneously free all sentient beings.

CHAPTER 19

Giving:
Chin-niu's Thanksgiving

There is usually an unwritten agreement that when we give we will get something in return. But is this really what giving is all about? In Buddhism there are four kinds of giving. There is spiritual giving—giving of one's practice, sharing the "dharma assets," giving of oneself for the ten thousand dharmas. There is also material giving, the giving of objects, where we give material things and wealth. In physical giving we give our labor, our physical presence; it is a giving of the body. There is also emotional giving, where we give our caring, our love—a giving of the heart.

Consider the giving involved in *oryoki,* the formal meal received in the zendo. We start off by reflecting on the life of the Buddha—his birth, enlightenment, teaching, and death. Then we open the "eating bowls of suchness," the Tathagata's eating bowls. This is followed by an invocation of the Buddhas. We chant the names of the

Buddha—Vairochana Buddha, pure Dharmakaya, numerous Nirmanakaya Buddhas, and the different bodhisattvas. This is followed by the meal gatha: "First, seventy-two labors brought us this food . . . we eat this food with everyone. We eat to stop all evil, to practice good, to save all sentient beings, and to accomplish the Buddha Way." This is reflection and thanksgiving.

In *oryoki* we express our gratitude to the Buddha and to the teachers, to our parents and genetic lineage, to all beings, to the ten thousand dharmas. We cannot receive unless we are willing to give, and we cannot give unless we are willing to receive. *Oryoki* is ended with a verse that the chant leader does alone: "May we exist in muddy water, with purity like a lotus. Thus we bow to Buddha." This is returning the meal, and our lives, with gratitude to all life.

Reflection and thanksgiving are the dharma food that we consume before the meal. It is very important to have that thanksgiving. The practice of gratitude is an essential aspect of our practice; otherwise we're just receiving all the time. It's important to give thanks, to recognize the unity of giver and receiver. Otherwise we become thieves. We just take, and there is no giving in return.

There is a koan in *The Blue Cliff Record* collection that looks at the heart of "reflection and thanksgiving." The main case says:

Every day at mealtime Master Chin-niu would personally take the rice pail and do a dance in front of the monastics' hall. Laughing aloud, he would say, "Bodhisattvas, come and eat!" Hsüeh-tou said, "Though he acted like this, Chin-niu is not good-hearted."

A monastic later asked Ch'ang-ch'ing, "When a man of old said, 'Bodhisattvas, come and eat!' what was his

*meaning?" Ch'ang-ch'ing said, "Reflection and thanks-
giving on the occasion of a meal."*

Chin-niu served a very special kind of dharma food
here. In the pointer to the main case, Yüan-wu talks about
it: "Wielding Manjushri's sword, he cuts off the nest of
trailing vines." Trailing vines are the things that obstruct
our way: all the creations made by the way we use our
minds, the way we respond to the universe. The way we
respond to moment-to-moment encounters in life ends up
creating all kinds of barriers: vines and entanglements.
Master Chin-niu, using Manjushri's sword—the sword of
wisdom—slices through this "nest of trailing vines."

The pointer continues: "Hanging a clear mirror on
high, he brings forth Vairochana's seal within a phrase."
This is the mirror of wisdom that reflects perfectly everything in front of it. When someone old is in front of it, it
reflects an old person; when someone young appears, it
reflects a young person. It doesn't superimpose anything
else on top of what is there. It just lets it be, as it is. Chin-
niu brings forth Vairochana's seal. Vairochana is the
Buddha of the Dharmakaya. When we chant, "Pure
Dharmakaya Vairochana Buddha," that's the dharma body
of the Buddha, Vairochana Buddha. Sambhogakaya
Buddha is the body of bliss, and Nirmanakaya is the "in the
world" manifestation, or the physical body, of the Buddha.

The pointer concludes: "Where one's state is secure
within, one wears clothes and eats food. Where spiritual
powers wander at play, how can one linger?" In other
words, when we are clear and complete within ourself,
then life goes on in a very ordinary way.

In the main case, the old teacher Chin-niu presents
us with this challenge: "Every day at mealtime, Master
Chin-niu would personally take the rice pail and do a

dance in front of the monastics' hall. Laughing aloud, he would say, 'Bodhisattvas, come and eat!'" One teacher, commenting on this, said, "He applies pure ghee and poison at the same time." Ghee is something wonderful in Asian cooking, held in very high regard and considered to have medicinal properties. At the same time as he brings out this wonderful ghee, he's applying poison. He's going to kill these monastics, in a way. He's going to nourish them and he's going to kill them, by killing their idea of a separate and distinct self. He's giving life to the reality that giver and receiver are one reality, not two things.

The main case continues: "Hsüeh-tou said, 'Though he acted like this, Chin-niu is not good-hearted.'" This is a thief recognizing a thief, a spirit recognizing a spirit. If a person comes talking of right and wrong, then that person is a person of right and wrong.

And then the final line: "A monastic later asked Ch'ang-ch'ing, 'When a man of old said, "Bodhisattvas, come and eat!" what was his meaning?' Ch'ang-ch'ing said, 'Reflection and thanksgiving on the occasion of a meal.'"

Master Chin-niu was one of the eighty outstanding disciples of the great Master Ma-tsu, at the height of the Tang dynasty golden age of Zen. The story goes that he would do his little dance with the pail of rice as a daily ritual. He did it every day for some twenty or more years. Always laughing, always inviting the monastics to take their meal. What was it all about? Was he just calling the others to come and eat?

Master Yüan-wu, commenting on this, says, "The ancient Chin-niu's expedient methods were just to make you directly receive it. Later, people would vainly calculate on their own and say, 'Why so many concerns? When it's cold, turn toward the fire. When it's hot, take advantage of the cool shade. When hungry, eat. When tired, get some sleep.'"

Yüan-wu goes on to say, "If we interpret its meaning this way, on the basis of ordinary feelings, to explain and comment, then the whole school of Bodhidharma would have been wiped off the face of the earth. Don't you realize that twenty-four hours a day, from moment to moment, the ancients never gave up wanting to understand this matter?" This is a warning against the "everything I do is Zen" syndrome.

Hsüeh-tou said, "Though he acted like this, Chin-niu is not good-hearted." Yüan-wu said, "Many people misunderstand this line. That which is called the supreme flavor of pure ghee is converted on encountering such people into poison." Since he descended into the weeds to help, why did Hsüeh-tou say that Chin-niu wasn't good-hearted? He was obviously showing compassion. Why would Hsüeh-tou say he wasn't good-hearted?

Being good-hearted, doing good, being a good person, is very different from compassion. In compassion there's no sense of an agent doing anything, nor of the action itself. There is no separation. Compassion happens. It happens the way you grow your hair, the way you sneeze when you have a tickle in your nose, the way you clear your throat, without even knowing that you're doing it. It's spontaneous and not preconceived. There's no expectation of reward or payoff. It's like taking care of yourself. When you have realized that self and other are not two separate things, compassion begins to function freely and easily.

Yüan-wu says, "People today don't get to the ancients' realm. They just say, 'What mind is there to see?' 'What Buddha is there?' If you construct such views, you've destroyed the Old Adept. To see Chin-niu, it takes thorough observation to begin to understand. If today and tomorrow you go on with such facile explanations, you'll never finish." How do you see Chin-niu, his joyful praise and thanksgiving on the occasion of a meal?

Master Dogen speaks of giving as one of the four activities of a bodhisattva. Giving is nongreed; nongreed is another way of saying compassion. The other side of greed is compassion. The other side of anger is wisdom. The other side of delusion is enlightenment. Greed, anger, and ignorance function as the three poisons because of the idea of a self, the idea that who we are is separate and distinct from the rest of the universe. Take away the self, forget the self, and those very same characteristics spontaneously manifest as the three virtues of compassion, wisdom, and enlightenment.

The other activities characterizing a bodhisattva as ennumerated by Dogen are loving speech, service for the welfare of others, and identity with others. Actually, identity with others should probably be listed first because when that's realized, everything else naturally follows. There is no question about loving speech, the welfare of others, or giving when you see self and other as the same reality. This is realizing that everything you do is the same as everything that happens to you. The dharma reaches everywhere, it fills the universe. There is no place outside it.

How does giving function amid the complexities and uncertainties of modern, real-life dilemmas? We are presented with opportunities to test that question every day. On a collective scale, as a monastery, we had a chance recently to practice this koan on the ecological frontier. We came to a head-to-head, eyeball-to-eyeball confrontation with a very formidable opponent, the Department of Environmental Conservation (DEC) of the state of New York.

They tried to get an easement on a piece of the land we own. In the easement they asked for all kinds of extraordinary privileges, such as the privilege to clear-cut the forest. The land in question is part of the nature sanctuary where we conduct workshops on the environment. A number of creatures on the endangered species list nest and feed there. We have had sightings of bald eagles, pileated woodpeckers, ospreys, and various hawks. The land connects with the rest of our two hundred acres. They wanted five acres so they could dredge and fill, put a road through, bring in heavy equipment—all that right in the middle of a fragile wetland ecosystem.

The DEC is formidable because they can bring to bear the force of the entire state. They have the law of eminent domain on their side. It allows them to obtain land despite an owner's unwillingness to sell. They've been acquiring land along the whole river to do flood control. But did they have to destroy a fragile environment in order to do this? We asked that question and they answered, "Yes, we do." So we resisted, and they did what they have a right to do. They started proceedings to condemn the land and take it anyway. In this koan we're talking about giving; what about looking a bit at taking? In this situation with the DEC, no permission was granted, there was no willingness on the part of the "giver." Taking is a unilateral action.

We took some immediate steps and drew up a plan. With a problem like this, the immediate response is to really personalize it. It's like somebody poking at your eyeball. Since I grew up on the streets, my first response was the street response, but that wasn't the end of it. My son had a similar reaction. He saw me going over the legal papers and wanted to know what was going on. I explained the situation to him. He was quiet for quite a while. I thought he'd forgotten about it, so I went back to what I was doing. Then, after a few minutes, he said, "Dad! I'm going to jail!" I asked "Why?" He said, "If someone starts cutting down those trees I'm going to kill them!" So we sat down and had a long discussion about alternative approaches to this problem. I told him about the various ecology groups and their different tactics. He loved Greenpeace. He loved the radicals, those who blow up the bulldozers and confront huge oil ships with little boats.

But there are other ways. In addition to the street-fighter response—which is rarely effective—we also had the possibility of just giving up and letting them do it. But we are the advocates of the insentient and sentient beings on this mountain. If the New York State Department of Environmental Conservation isn't going to take care of the bald eagle and the pileated woodpecker and the timber rattler, who's going to do it?

When we first came to Mount Tremper, our first action was to give the land back to the wilderness. We did that with a proclamation of the monastery Board of Directors. Eighty percent of the land is to remain forever wild. We would live on twenty percent of it as custodians, with the land on loan to us. It still belongs to the environment, to all beings. If we don't speak up for them, if we don't do something, who will? The deer, the porcupines, the racoons, don't have anyone else. In light of that, giving up seemed not a very compassionate alternative.

We could compromise. We could say, "Okay, take part of it." But whatever our willingness might be, they would proceed to do whatever they wanted to do. They had right and might on their side. The most we could do is create a little diversion for them and, maybe, get some concessions along the way.

In negotiating with them, I asked, "What about

separation of church and state? Here's the state coming and taking church property." Their representative said, "Oh, we've done that before." He said that big companies have tried to resist them and weren't successful. "We just put them in court and they see that it's costing them more money in lawyers' fees than the thing is worth, and they give up. We get what we want, so it is pointless and wasteful to fight us. Don't even think about it. You will do yourself a favor." I said, "Well, we have a number of lawyers who are students here. They sit zazen ten hours a day for weeks on end. They have lots of patience."

We could also get creative. We found out that one of the state DEC officials was hoping to get appointed to a position with the Environmental Protection Agency of the federal government. Obviously, the last thing he wanted was to be known as someone who takes away the nesting place of the pileated woodpecker and the bald eagle. We could just dress up in our robes and take picket signs to the state capital. Get some media coverage. The newspapers would love it.

What to do? All of these possibilities that I've mentioned are about winning and losing. The dharma, this incredible dharma, is not about winning or losing. Dharma combat is not about winning or losing. It's about practice, about doing. It's about making realization our own. It's about giving realization away to all sentient beings. There are no success stories, no rewards, no recognition.

How does that relate to a problem like the conflict with the DEC? If it's not about winning or losing, what is it about? How do we deal with someone taking that which is not freely given? We might ask ourselves the question, What can we give to the DEC? What can we give to the thief in the night?

Ryokan, the Zen poet, had a little hermitage in the

mountains. One freezing-cold December night, while he was gone, a thief broke in but could find nothing to steal. Ryokan was an accomplished pauper. When he returned, he surprised the thief. He felt so bad that the thief had found nothing to steal that he took off his robes and gave them to the thief. The thief left and Ryokan, sitting by the window, shivering and looking at the full moon over the mountain, said, "Ah, such a beautiful moon. If only I could have given him that."

What can we give to the thief? What can we offer, not just to the hungry, the homeless, the dying, the beggar, but to the thief, the warlord, the rapists of women and the environment, the crooked politicians, land developers, child abusers? What can we give them?

We can give the self. And we can give the self just for the sake of giving the self. We can give loving speech. Master Dogen said, "Loving speech means that as you meet sentient beings you first arouse a sense of compassion in your mind and treat them with considerate, affectionate words. Praise the virtuous, have compassion for the wicked. As you take delight in affectionate words, they will gradually flourish. And then even those loving words that were unknown to you, and unperceived by you, will be revealed to you." Just by the practice of loving speech, it all begins to unfold. Zazen begets zazen, enlightenment begets enlightenment. When the first thought springs from enlightenment, all subsequent thoughts are enlightened. Compassionate speech is fundamental to the pacification of enemies.

Dogen continued, "You should ponder that thoughtful words arise from the mind of loving-kindness. The mind of loving-kindness has compassion as its seed. Consider this: the loving speech of remonstrance." Remonstrance means to plead in opposition to something, to speak in protest or reproof, to vigorously reject or oppose. He's saying that the loving speech of vigorously opposing "has the power to influence even the emperor's mind." If it can influence the emperor's mind, maybe the DEC commissioner might respond to loving speech as well.

Dogen added, "Working for the welfare of all beings means that you contrive ways to benefit all sentient beings, high and low." We tend to think that when we work for the benefit of all beings, it's always someone lower than us who receives the benefits. We rarely see ourselves reaching up to someone higher than us, more fortunate than us, more powerful than us, and working for their welfare, giving them loving speech, giving anything to them. Instead, we fight them.

Dogen concluded, "Commiserate with the turtle in trouble; take care of the sparrow suffering from injury." When we see a distressed turtle or watch a sick sparrow, we don't expect any repayment for our favors but are moved entirely by our desire to help. Can we experience this kind of desire to help others when we are dealing with the enemy, with the opposition, with the other side? Can we possibly give loving-kindness and loving speech to that or those which oppose and confront us? First, give the self. Give the self for the sake of giving. Not for any reward, just for the desire to help, to give. Let the Way manifest through itself. That's what giving the self is about. Giving is nonattachment.

Master Hsüeh-tou's verse to this koan looks again at Chin-niu's giving.

> *Laughing aloud in the shadow of the white clouds,*
> *He lifts it up with both hands to give it to them.*
> *If they were children of the golden-haired lion,*
> *They would have seen the deception from three*
>   *thousand miles away.*

Laughing aloud in the shadow of the white clouds . . .
Is this thanksgiving on the occasion of a meal? *He lifts it up with both hands to give it to them.* He is not speaking here of just the rice; there is something else that is being given. What is the dharma food that Chin-niu is serving with that meal of rice? That is what we need to see in this koan. If you see it, you're one of those golden-haired lions, according to Yüan-wu, and there's no need then for Chin-niu to continue his dance.

If you see it, you would immediately recognize the deception from three thousand miles away. What's the deception? How is Chin-niu deceiving these monastics? We need to see it from the perspective of Chin-niu. We need to appreciate it from the perspective of the monastics. It is always important in this practice to function outside of the patterns. If we just go to the words and the actions, we're going to miss it. What is going on outside of the patterns? What is the dharma food of Chin-niu?

We need to appreciate that all this giving is an aspect of the bodhisattva's vow to save all sentient beings, the vow to postpone our own enlightenment until every last person has realized it, the vow to serve the welfare of others, the vow of loving-kindness.

We tend to look at giving in the conventional way: that when you give, you receive, and think that that's what "giving and receiving are one" really means. That's not what it means. It means the giver and the receiver are the same thing. It doesn't mean that when you give something, you're going to receive something. Ultimately, there is no giving and there is no receiving.

If we begin to construct ideas about the good that we're going to get by giving, we've missed the point of *dana*, the true giving. We tend to see our practice with the same misconception—that what our practice is about is our liberation, our enlightenment. But the dharma is non-dual. The actions of a bodhisattva are selfless activities. They're undefiled, free, natural, not self-centered. Individual liberation is a contradiction in terms. How could there possibly be individual liberation? "All sentient beings and I at once attain the Way" is what the Buddha said when he realized himself. And so it is for everybody.

Enlightenment is not a solitary thing. The Diamond Net of Indra includes the whole catastrophe—demons and gods, crooks and saints, you and me. It's all the same catastrophe. How could there be individual liberation? Liberation can only be fulfilled in the context of the liberation of all beings; it is social liberation, if you will. And it includes *all* beings, sentient and insentient. That's the only way any of us will ever realize complete liberation.

Paramita means "to cross over to the other shore." We should understand that "to cross over to the other shore" is the other shore's arriving here. "Saving all sentient beings" is being saved by all sentient beings. If we're not prepared to be saved by all sentient beings, there's no way that we can save all sentient beings. That's what the Dalai Lama was speaking of when he referred to Mao Zedong as one of his great teachers. Mao Zedong is responsible for the destruction of Tibet, the deaths of millions of people, the eradication of a culture and a religion. His image, years after his death, is still wreaking havoc on the Dalai Lama's country and his people. Yet the Dalai Lama says, with loving-kindness, "He's my greatest teacher." The other shore arrives.

If you don't understand, study and practice this matter. It's a key part of our training. It's the interface that we make with the world. We've got a habitual way of dealing with the world, a way that is self-centered, that comes from our conditioning. This practice is an opportunity to turn it over and see it from all sides, an opportunity to take care of the things that need taking care of in a way that's not self-centered, that doesn't oppose this over that but sees the whole thing as an interacting totality that affects everything. It's only in this way that we can nourish and heal ourselves and the environment.

We may lose control of the land to the DEC. "We"—the fish and the fowl and the mammals and the wildflowers—may lose that land, and we may not. Ultimately, either way is okay. But we must, we *must*, confront the issues, take up the challenge as it's presented to us. You may never realize yourself. But you must practice. Not for the goal but for each moment.

The point is not winning or losing, gain or loss. There is no gain or loss. It is like dokusan. When you don't pass a koan, it doesn't mean that you give up and say, "Oh, I can't pass koans." It doesn't mean that you get angry. It means that you didn't see that koan, and you go back and you sit, and you do it again. And you're sent back and you go back again. And you're sent back and you go back again. This is your practice. It's no big deal. You're not a hero for doing it. You're doing it because you are who you are, or you wouldn't be studying the self. You practice, not because of me, but because of you. And when you realize that "you," you realize the whole universe.

PART III

Questions and Answers

CHAPTER 20

Questions and Answers:
From an Evening at the Monastery

Q. Can you elaborate on what you mean when you say that giving the precepts is very personal to you?

A. What you are saying is true. Giving the precepts is very personal, not only for me but also for the student. I have found them to be one of the most profound teachings we have, and the one most likely to impact not only the student's life but the lives of everyone that student comes in contact with. They are also personal because of the lineage of ancestors who have handed them down from generation to generation.

In the transmission of the dharma from teacher to student there is a series of teachings toward the very end of formal training called *denkai*. *Kai* means precepts. Transmission of the precepts is a verification of the fact that the student has realized and actualized those precepts in his or her own life. This is different from receiving the precepts in jukai. In *denkai* your teacher, after testing your understanding of the precepts with 120 koans, begins to give you a series of oral teachings on the precepts and on how to do certain priestly functions. You become part of that lineage of transmitting the precepts.

When you give the precepts to a student, you give the student a lineage chart on which are written all the names of the ancestors who have passed down these precepts, beginning with Shakayamuni Buddha. The names are written in a huge circle, with the student's name next to the teacher's name on the chart. That circle is not just the circle of those ancestors. It includes the whole phenomenal universe. It is the pure Dharmakaya. Nothing is left out. In taking the precepts you are becoming part of that family of practitioners who have vowed to practice those precepts in their lives. *That* is very personal.

Q. Why are so many people these days becoming Buddhists?

A. I don't know. I know why I did but I don't know about anyone else. Sometimes we don't know ourselves why we did something. When I press students on why they want to become a Buddhist, I ask them to reflect on this personally. It is important for students to be clear on what they aspire to, what their motivation is, and how to cultivate it.

To me the "cultivator of cultivators" is zazen. I trust zazen. I trust zazen because I was probably the most deluded, confused, angry, antireligious person you could ever meet. There is no reason in heaven or hell why I should be a Zen teacher, sitting here, talking like this. All I know is I found out about zazen. In the beginning I did very little sitting. Every time I finished a period of zazen, I cursed it. I said it was stupid, a waste of time. My legs hurt, yet the next day I would find myself sitting again. The more I sat, the deeper I went.

Initially I was practicing because I wanted to take better pictures. At that time I was a professional photographer, and my photography teacher, Minor White, told me that meditation helped him to "see" more clearly. I wanted to "see" like Minor White saw, and if he had stood on his head, I would have stood on my head! Fortunately, he did meditation. So that is what I took up. And it took me to the next step, and that took me to the next step, and finally I reached a point where, instead of fighting every step, I just relaxed into it and allowed it to unfold. Zazen cultivates itself; that is why it is the cultivator of cultivators.

Q. I get confused trying to figure out whether I should work with the precepts consciously, by thinking about them, and then acting, or should I just let my actions be more spontaneous and trust that the precepts will be the basis for how I act?

A. That is a problem that students also face in the Zen arts. When a *sumi-e* master does a painting, he is not thinking about it. He doesn't say, "Okay, I'll put the tail of the ox here, and now about this far over the horns go . . ." He just opens up into the painting. It pours out of him. It is totally unconscious. But that comes from years and years of painting bamboo leaves and butterflies, with the teacher continuously saying, "Not good enough. More, more." It is the same way with the martial arts. Somebody grabs you from behind, and you explode into a proper response. You cannot do that consciously. It is totally unconscious. It happens after years and years and years of practice, doing each *kata* over and over again, until it becomes one with you.

In practicing the precepts, a similar thing happens. They are received at the beginning of training on faith. It is in the years of dokusans that follow, the years of practicing the precepts, realizing that we are violating them, taking responsibility, and returning to the precepts, that they begin to sink in deeper and deeper. They begin to penetrate every fiber of our being—every cell in our body begins to manifest those precepts. By the time training is over, and the kai are transmitted, the student should really understand the vital workings of these precepts. It is a subtle process, and you have to be careful that you don't delude yourself.

Q. How do I keep my practice of the precepts fresh?

A. One of the ways in which the members of our sangha in Greenhaven Maximum Security Prison keep their practice of the precepts alive is by conducting a short service in which they recite the precepts, reading them from the "Kyojukaimon," following morning zazen each day. This was their own idea. They have no personal altars. They are not even allowed *zafus*. To sit zazen they use a rolled-up blanket. They are not allowed to congregate early in the morning, so they sit and recite the precepts in their cells. Day after day they continue to recite the precepts, and this helps to keep their practice alive.

Q. When students have completed formal training and have understood the precepts, is their understanding relative? Could two students, both of whom have finished training, come to two different conclusions on what the precept Do not kill *means? Would both of them be right, or is there one absolute right answer?*

A. Good and evil, by their very nature, exist in the world of the relative. There is no way to talk about them other than in the relativistic sense. Two farmers have farms right beside each other. One has just finished harvesting his crop of grapes, and they are lying on racks in the sun, drying, becoming raisins. The farmer next door has just finished plowing his field and putting seed in the ground. The ground is very dry, and the seed needs moisture to sprout. One is praying for sunlight, the other is praying for rain. It starts raining. The one who put the seed in says, "Thank you, God, for the rain. It's good." The other one says, "Damn you, God, the rain is destroying my raisins! They're going to mildew, and I'm not going to be able to sell them." Same rain, but the relative position is quite different.

Someone points a gun at me—bad karma. They shoot, I duck—good karma. The bullet hits you—bad karma for you. For me it is good karma. Same bullet, relative views.

The question that naturally arises out of this is, How can we know how to function? Is it ever right to kill? Under what circumstances? By the time a student has completed formal training, he or she will have done more than 800 koans. Included in these 800 koans are the 120 koans that specifically examine the sixteen precepts from every possible perspective—from an absolute perspective, from a perspective of compassion and reverence for life, and from a literal understanding of the precept.

The wonderful thing about these precepts is that they are not fixed rules of action. They allow for changes in circumstances: for adjusting to the time, the particular place, your position, and the degree of action necessary in any given situation. What is appropriate at one time may not be appropriate at another. Times change, and it is important that we respond sensitively to the changes. The same is true regarding place. To wear my abbot's robe at the monastery is appropriate; to wear it to the local diner is not. There is nothing wrong with the robe, but the meaning of its use changes from place to place.

One's position in the context of a situation also influences action. What I do as a teacher, as a parent, or as a lover varies significantly. What is right in one role is way out of line in another. For each of us our relative position has to be considered. How much action is called for? Sometimes a whisper is sufficient; at another time a shout may be best. Each of the senior students in your question will have his or her own unique course of action in any given situation.

Q. I have heard some people justify their actions from the so-called absolute perspective, by saying that there is no good and evil. This is used as justification for behaving in a manner that I find disturbing.

A. The fact is, there is good and evil. Emptiness, or the absolute, is one side, and the world of phenomena, or the relative, is the other side. The truth is to be found in neither of those. Tweak the nose of the person who says he or she is absolute, beyond good and evil. Ask if it hurts.

Q. Are good and evil something innate in us? If they are, then doesn't that imply that regardless of whether we have taken the precepts or not, our responses to situations and people will be coming from one or the other of those two extremes?

A. The basis of the precepts is that evil is something you have to create. It takes action, it takes activity to do it. But good is also something you have to create. It also takes action or activity. The moment you have activity, you have karma, and you have good and evil.

From an absolute perspective there is neither good

nor evil. With this in mind, how will a person naturally respond? Well, the precepts are based on a realization. When you receive them on the basis of faith at the beginning of your training, they are based on the realization of the Buddha, or your teacher, who is saying, "These work. This is good." Eventually, they must become your own realization. And what is that realization? The realization is that the ten thousand things and I are the same reality. The realization is that what I do and what happens to me are the same thing. I can't do anything to anything without doing it to myself, because "that" thing is me. Because I am the whole universe. I want to take care of it like I want to take care of my body. I don't want it to be hurt. I don't want a hole in the ozone layer any more than I want a hole in my head. It becomes a very personal matter.

The precepts are about creating activity in the world in a way that is in harmony with it. It is what we call compassion. The first realization—you and I are the same thing—is wisdom, the realization of the oneness. The manifestation of that wisdom in the world of separation—the world of "I am not you and you are not me"— is compassion, which is the functioning of the precepts.

Q. *Why does the second pure precept say "practice good" rather than "practice love" or "practice compassion?"*

A. The precepts are moral and ethical values. They are guidelines to practice. Love is different. Define love for me. What is it? Whose definition will you use for it? Hallmark greeting cards'? Hollywood's? There is a reason for not using the word *love*. It is because of all the associations that go along with it. People say it all the time. "I love you, honey!" It loses all its meaning, and it has become a catchphrase in our society. We use it to sell everything from perfume to cars to condoms. What does it really mean? Is the love that a mother has for a child and the love that a man has for a woman the same? Is the love that a woman has for a woman, and a man for a man the same? Is the love of nature the same as the love of self? Love is a very broad condition that really is aside from moral and ethical values. It is a nice thing, but it is just half a degree this side of hate, as we can see quite frequently. Keep in mind that in most instances of rape and wife battering, the perpetrator is the woman's lover or husband.

Q. How do I know in a given situation if what I am doing is really for the best?

A. All I know is that in any situation, individuals need to respond in accord with what they see they can do, and with the information available to them at the time. Fifteen years ago, some local people arranged an airdrop of hay bales for the wild deer during a very deep snow because the deer were all dying of starvation. But in the winter, deer feed on the bark of trees, and their digestive system is no longer capable of assimilating hay. So, unable to digest the hay they had eaten, their stomachs produced a lot of gas. We found these bloated, dead deer all over the mountain. Probably more deer were killed by the consequences of that action than the winter would have killed. Yet, that obviously was not the intent.

Q. With the example of the deer, the people's intention was good, yet the deer died. How does the role of intent relate to the creation of karma?

A. The intent was fine. But there was still the consequences of the action. No matter what you do with these precepts, and you could be completely abiding by them, there may be consequences to your actions that are negative because of reasons you are unaware of. Let's say you help an old woman cross the street, and for no reason that you can see, she starts slapping you, "Get your hands off me, get away from me." The next thing you know a cop comes and arrests you, and all you were trying to do was to help an old woman across the street! The intention was good, yet these are the consequences. Here we confront the difference between a do-gooder and true compassion. In true compassion there is intimacy—that is, no separation. That intimacy brings a particular kind of sensitivity to the situation that goes beyond the drive to simply do good. It is more intuitive and insightful.

Q. I know a lot of people who are unwilling to face issues of power in their lives and want to hand over power to someone else, especially in the teacher-student relationship. What do the precepts have to say about the misuse or use of power?

A. First of all, shame on people who accept power from someone else. They are not really helping anybody. This occurs in Zen training all the time. People want to give over control to their teacher in a way similar to what happens in traditions where a teacher functions like a guru. A guru uses the power handed to him to help the student. We don't have a guru-student relationship in Zen, so when students come along and want to give away their power, a Zen teacher will throw it right back at them. But there is definitely a hierarchy; ask anyone who has been to a Zen center. The hierarchy is not necessarily evil, unless it is used in that way. I think it makes all the difference in the world how power or hierarchy is used. Somebody with a lot of money is not necessarily evil, particularly if he or she uses that money for the benefit of others and is generous with it. But if that power is used for self-gratification or self-advancement and not for the benefit of others, it violates the precepts.

Q. How does the practice of the precepts apply when somebody close to me is talking about someone else in a derogatory fashion? Do I have a responsibility to make that person aware of what he or she is doing?

A. The bottom line is that these precepts are yours. You should maintain and practice them, not be someone else's uninvited spiritual conscience. On the other hand, it is not so simple. The precept you are talking about, *Not speaking of others' errors and faults,* needs to be appreciated from the literal point of view: don't ever speak of anybody's errors and faults. It should also be appreciated from the point of view of reverence for life and compassion: when necessary you must speak out. And from the point of view of the absolute—who will speak of what, since there is only you in the whole universe? To even give rise to the thought of "other" violates the precept. From the perspective of reverence for life, and compassion, if you witness somebody doing something wrong, a rape, for example, and the police ask, "Did anybody see it?" and because you don't want to speak of anybody's errors and faults, you don't say anything, you violate the precept—particularly if you do that to save yourself: "I don't want to say anything because that person's going to do me in, or his brother is, or his friends are." That is self-centered and definitely violates the precept. Even if you are putting yourself at risk, you have a moral responsibility to say something.

Q. In the city where I live, seven children were left by themselves at night. Their parents were addicts. They left the kids, the oldest of whom was seven, alone in the house. A fire broke out, and the oldest child, who was like a mother to all the children, led them to a window, where she thought they could escape. But the window was barred, and they all perished in the fire. How does something like that happen. Is it karma?

A. I remember reading about that incident. Karma, from a Buddhist perspective, is ongoing. There is an individual's karma. There is the karma of a family. There is karma that we have created right here by being together. There is the karma of a race, of a culture. I feel that our country has created an incredible karma by what we did to establish ourselves in this country to begin with—what we did to Native Americans, what we did to the Africans, what we did to each generation of the poor and hungry that came to these shores. In spite of our message on the Statue of Liberty, we made it a living hell for them. You can imagine the karma of a young Jewish baby born at the time of the Holocaust. An innocent child, but the karma of its parents was its karma.

In fact, in Buddhism we say that we choose our parents, that birth is not an accident. *The Tibetan Book of the Dead* describes how there is a force looking for a body to be born into. When the appropiate circumstances appear, it takes on a new birth. It is the volition of that spirit, that energy, that causes the birth. So, in a sense, you give birth to yourself. Karma always begins to isolate itself when you isolate yourself. The fact is that, whether we realize it or not, each one of us is the Diamond Net of Indra that pervades the whole universe. Birth is the unborn, and death is the unextinguished. There is no one that is born, and there is no one that dies. But the minute you isolate yourself and say, "Yes, I'm this bag of skin," there is a lot of karma connected with that bag of skin.

And that karma is not only our personal karma but that of our family, parents, nation, even the street we live on. It can be very painful.

I look at my kids. One is thirty-eight now, one is thirty-seven, and one is twenty-one. I see them manifest things that create the same pain in their lives that I remember from my own, the things I used to do, the way I saw things. Now it is their karma, and there is nothing I can do about it. All we can do is be aware and take responsibility where and when we can.

Q. If a woman discovers that there is a life growing inside her, and she decides that she does not want to be pregnant and spend the next twenty years caring for a child, other people or society becomes involved and tells her that she has no right to make that decision, or that she is wrong. What do Zen and the precepts have to say in this situation?

A. From a Buddhist perspective, making that choice, and the consequences of that choice, are the woman's, as is every single decision that you make with regard to the precepts. We don't have a pope, yet, in Zen, and I am not the interpreter of precepts for people. Each person has to weigh the consequences individually, and each person will bear the karma of his or her decisions, good or bad.

One of the students here is a physician. He had to carry out the decision of withdrawing life support on a brain-dead baby whose whole family was killed, except for the father. New York State law requires that the hospital recognize the parent's wish in a case like that. The hospital lawyers agreed, the parent agreed, so the final decision was made. The life-support machines were to be switched off and the baby's organs donated to another hospital to help the life of another infant. The physician, who had just recently received the precepts, was having a very hard time carrying out this decision.

He called me up and said, "What do you do in a case like this?" I said to him over the phone, "You know that it's your decision. They're your precepts, not mine. You understand how they function. There will be karmic consequences. You have a responsibility to the dharma, you have a responsibility to the hospital, and to the parent. I'm not a doctor. I'm not in that position. You're the only one that really knows how to make this decision." He made the decision and pulled the plug. A doctor who had come from another hospital to pick up the organs was standing there with an icebox waiting for the organs. That made the whole situation more ghoulish.

A couple of the nurses became upset enough to bring charges against the physician who switched off the life support. This was one of the karmic consequences of his action. Was it a good action; was it a bad action? Did it uphold the precepts? Was the physician acting in self-interest? It definitely wasn't his self-interest. His preference would have been not to deal with it at all. The charges were eventually dropped. Karmic consequences always follow, regardless of what the action is. It is in the hands of whoever did it, whoever took the action. Returning to the focus of your question, it would be in the woman's hands.

Q. What if someone pushes a child out of the way of an oncoming train and gets hit instead. The person upheld the life of the child but not his or her own. What would the consequences of that action be?

A. The person dies! And if I were the other person, the one who was saved, I would make a vow, then and there, while the corpse was still warm, that I would do something to repay the life given for me. For example, if the person had a family, I would support the family.

Q. *How about if you failed to shove the other person out of the way? You could have done it but you knew that it would have been at the expense of your own life. How could you possibly make a decision like that?*

A. This is a tough one. Not many people would do it. But there are people who will risk their lives for another person. It happens all the time. When they take the risk they don't even think about it. They may experience a feeling of invulnerability. Take the example of a fireman who charges into a burning building to rescue a person who is trapped. He understands fire. It is his business. It is a calculated risk. It is a different risk than climbing a mountain or skydiving. Those are risks that are taken just for the sheer thrill of it, and as Gary Synder says, "Primitive people would never do that." Life is enough of a thrill without making it any worse! I have nothing but absolute gratitude to the police, the good ones. If there is a gunshot, the logical reaction for most people is to run in the opposite direction. The police run toward the gunfire. That is opposed to any sane person's natural instinct. When people take risks of that kind, it has to do with something much deeper than any kind of logic.

I remember watching the TV news coverage of the plane that hit a bridge and went down in the Potomac River in Washington. There was a stewardess in the river, and the helicopters had a spotlight and cameras focused right on her. It was winter and snowing heavily. She was struggling, swimming, desperately trying to reach the bank. A bunch of people were on shore, encouraging her, throwing her life rings, but they were all out of reach. Suddenly she disappears under the waves and then surfaces again, struggling to remain afloat. Then some bystander, not a fireman, just some guy standing on the shore, stripped and jumped in. He swam to the stewardess and managed to save her. I am sure he wasn't reflecting on it. I am sure that his action came from someplace very deep within him. He was basically that kind of a person. I don't know if you can cultivate that. He wasn't being a bod-hisattva. He was really just being himself at the gut level.

Q. *The Gatha of Atonement seems to say that greed, anger, and ignorance are the root cause of all our karma, all our actions. Yet I feel that fear plays a large part in how I live my life. Where do you think fear comes from?*

A. Greed, anger, and ignorance are the root cause, not of all karma, but only of evil karma. I would say that fear comes out of ignorance, out of separation. Basically, fear has to do with what is going to happen next. It rarely has to do with the moment. It's "What's around the next corner, what's down the dark alley, what if I do this, what if I don't do that?" What if, what if, what if? If you come into the moment, there is no fear; the moment is quite different. It is expectation that creates our fear.

Q. *Is the precept* Honor the body: do not misuse sexuality, *just about sexuality?* Honor the body *seems much broader—sleeping well, eating well, not smoking, whatever.*

A. Originally, in the Theravadin *vinaya* (monastic rules), it was about celibacy. There was to be no expression of sexuality, period. If you look at the precept as it is worded in the early Mahayana scriptures, it is about not committing adultery. I added *Honor the body* as a way of showing the other side of not misusing sexuality, of not just treating the body as a sexual object but also honoring it.

Q. What about masturbation? It seems to me to be utterly self-centered.

A. Masturbation is definitely self-centered, and because it is immediate gratification, it is very easy to get hooked on it. My feeling is that if you are in a relationship and masturbation keeps you from really making the best of that relationship—in other words, the self-gratification is better than the gratification in the relationship—then you are misusing sexuality. If you do not have a relationship, sometimes it is a way of maintaining sanity.

Q. How do you understand the difference between the vinaya's *insistence on complete celibacy and the Zen Mahayana precept* Do not misuse sexuality?

A. *Do not misuse sexuality* is a much broader statement than the one on celibacy. First of all, it is condoning sexuality. There are reasons for celibacy. When you look back through religious history, you can see that celibacy has been an integral part of many people's spiritual practice. It is something I wrestled with, and tried, for a couple of years. And maybe I could have practiced it if I had never experienced sex, but at thirty-five years of age to suddenly decide "Okay, now I'm going to be celibate" was tough. Sexual energy is energy. Energy is energy. *Ki* is *ki*. When you have it in your *hara* and you direct it across your knuckles, as in karate, you can break boards with it. When you put it into Mu, or another koan, you can see the koan. When it drops into your sexual organs, it is lust. It is the same energy. And if you learn how to transmute that energy, how to deal with that energy—which is what tantra is about—it becomes spiritual energy, a very powerful energy for people, one of the strongest.

That transformation of energy, in my opinion, is the

basis for celibacy in the religious traditions. But my feeling is that in this day and age, given the circumstances of our society in twentieth-century America, it is a very difficult practice. The issues the Catholic Church is now facing in terms of the low numbers of men joining the priesthood or women entering the convents is a good indication of that. For us at the monastery, it is an option. Our monastics can either take a vow of celibacy or have a stable binary relationship. And that stable binary relationship does not preclude gay relationships.

Q. In the Gatha of Atonement that we chant during the renewal of precepts ceremony, it says, "All evil karma committed by me since of old, on account of my beginningless greed, anger, and ignorance, born of my body, mind and thought—now I atone for it all." If I understand it correctly, this is saying that karma can be created by action, speech, and thought. Would this mean that fantasies invading somebody's sexual space would be a violation of the precept Do not misuse sexuality?

A. Yes, it is a violation of the precept and it has karmic consequences. If you sit there fantasizing about having sex with someone who is trying to talk to you, that is invading the person's space with thoughts. Lusting after someone, even though you are not saying or doing anything, is creating that kind of atmosphere. This is what leads to sexual harassment, which has its own karmic consequences. The human mind is a very powerful thing, and it is boundless. It communicates beyond words, beyond physical actions.

Q. I guess sexual harassment would also arise when a sexualized environment was created where sexual activity is not the purpose of the environment—a space where pictures of naked women or men are hanging, and you can't go into that space without entering the sexual thought realm.

A. Right. I often wonder how women feel when they go into a garage, and there are all these pictures of naked women hanging around.

Q. *Is monogamy or a long-term relationship essential to keeping the precept on not misusing sexuality?*

A. It helps because a commitment, an agreement, is what makes the world work. It is how we begin to trust people. There is nothing wrong with relationships that are not monogamous, but the rule still holds that it should be by mutual consent, so that a person is not just using his or her partner, not just handing out a line, "I love you, baby," and then disappearing after the encounter.

Q. *I have a question on the precept* Actualize harmony: do not be angry. *As a child I was taught that it was wrong to express certain feelings, especially anger. So even though on the surface I was very polite, inside I could be seething. Then three years ago I decided to change and manifest whatever I feel. Sometimes I am not proud of what I manifest, but it is what I am feeling at that moment, and it seems more honest than hiding it. In looking at the precept, I find myself bouncing between these two sides: Should I express my anger or should I keep it down and walk around with a "serene" look when that's not what I am feeling?*

A. What you are doing is straining yourself in order to be harmonious. When I first went to live at a Zen center full-time, I had already been practicing seriously for a number of years. So everybody expected me, or I thought they all expected me, to be the serene manifestation of the Bodhisattva Avalokiteshvara, the bodhisattva of compassion. Yet, I was angry most of the time. I remember walking down the street one day, really angry, and I saw my teacher coming up the street. I put this smile on my face and said, "Good morning." He said, "Good morning," and we walked past each other, and then suddenly I heard him call me, "Daido!" I turned around, and he made a straining face and grunted, "Gruhhhhhhh!" He saw right through me. I realized that the effort it took to fake it when I was feeling angry wasn't worth it. Maybe the effort I was putting into being serene should have been directed into dealing with the anger—experiencing it, not venting or suppressing it, but dealing with it. That is what I suggest to you.

Q. *When I am expressing the anger, I am dealing with it that way.*

A. But how about everybody else who is catching the fallout? Have a little compassion for them.

Q. *I do. I actually do.*

A. But compassion means you are doing something about it. Take responsibility for your action and let it go.

Q. *I am trying my best to do that but . . .*

A. You can't do it by suppressing it, and you can't do it by exploding with it. There is another way.

Q. *What is the other way then?*

A. The other way is to let go. Let go. Realize that when you reach the point where your nostrils are flaring and your eyes have rolled back into your head so you see only the whites, and drool is running out of the corner of your mouth and your face is red—when you've reached that point, it is too late. You have got to get to the place where the first thought arises, when the button is pushed.

Bink! A thought arises, and that immediately creates a second thought, and a third thought, a fourth thought, a fifth thought, and there is a chain reaction of thoughts that goes *[snaps fingers]* just like that, until finally you have the physiological reaction that you call anger. Adrenaline is pumping through your veins and you just pop your adversary right in the nose and deck him. But that has consequences. If you can get to the first thought, or to the place before the first thought, then there is something you can do about it. Because it has not yet manifested enough energy to do anything. That is where you can acknowledge it, take responsibility for it, and let go of it. Use your anger as a teacher.

Q. *Does that mean that I should allow a situation that is making me angry to continue, while I am working on my anger, dealing with it by letting go?*

A. Situations don't make you angry—you make you angry. That is the first step. I am angry because I made myself angry. He didn't make me angry. It didn't make me angry. I made me angry. Now you are full of the power to do something about anger.

Q. *But what if a person is being abusive to me? Aren't they making me angry?*

A. No, you are making you angry. You are listening to the abuse and creating the anger with your mind. You don't have to create the anger.

Q. *But shouldn't we take action if we see someone abusing an animal or a child?*

A. You don't have to be angry. You don't have to hate the deer to keep them out of your garden. You can take action without being angry. Unfortunately, much of our activity in the peace movement in this country stems from anger. We have unconsciously taken the Judeo-

Christian principle of "an eye for an eye and a tooth for a tooth" as a model upon which to base our actions.

It is only recently that we have begun to see that Buddhism has something to teach about how to demonstrate nonviolently, about how to be political without being angry. It does not mean that those other ways don't effect change, but it is important to know that there are other ways. It always rankles me when I hear people say that Gandhi and Martin Luther King were nonviolent. People were killed. You cannot go marching into a bunch of soldiers who have guns and say that what is happening is not violent. They are going to shoot you. And the soldiers did, they opened fire, and people were killed. In the end both Gandhi and King died a violent death. It doesn't mean that what they did wasn't important, or shouldn't be done, but to call it nonviolent misses the point. Nonviolent action springs from a place of no separation. When you see that the one in opposition is no other than yourself, then your response is very different. Your action comes from a place of compassion rather than angry confrontation.

Q. *What if someone is trying to harm me physically or mentally and in trying to prevent that I hurt him or her?*

A. You violate the precept. In kung fu, even though you may have lethal power, if you are attacked, you run away. If you can't run away, you avoid. You do this dance so they can't get you. If you can't avoid, you disarm; take the weapon away from them. If you can't disarm, you maim, to slow them down. The last resort is to kill, to use your power in a lethal way. If you do that to protect yourself, you violate the precept, because it is a self-centered action. If you do that to protect someone else, you uphold the precept.

Q. *When we talk about the precept* Proceed clearly: do not cloud the mind, *are thoughts included in that or is that just carrying it to a puritanical extreme?*

A. This particular precept is about intoxicating substances, such as alcohol or drugs.

Q. *When I lived at another Zen center, after a retreat my teacher would let some of the students buy wine and pot. Once he asked me to grow some pot, and I said no because I'm a recovering person. I didn't understand that anything that your teacher requests, you are supposed to do.*

A. Where did you hear that? You did the right thing.

Q. *But that made a problem in our relationship.*

A. Good. Rule number one—trust yourself. Okay?

Q. *You say that it is the same thing to break the precept in action, word, and thought, but it seems to me that it is worse to break it in action than it is to break it in thought.*

A. It is just more obvious. That's all. You just haven't realized how powerful your mind is yet. Not just your mind—anybody's mind. The human mind is an incredible vehicle. None of us, even in our wildest dream, can imagine the edges of its power, and probably no one has accessed it all, including our greatest geniuses. There is so much of it that we don't understand and probably will never understand.

Q. *The bluntest way of rephrasing this question is, once you have broken a precept in thought, why not break it in action as well?* [laughter]

A. Listen, you can justify yourself however you want, but however you cut it, it is the same karma.

Q. Are the karmic consequences of breaking any one of the precepts the same, or is there a different amount of karmic consequence?

A. The consequence of breaking any precept is the illusion of the self. It is a self-centered action. So that is the same for all of them. But obviously, the consequences of killing a person and of telling a white lie on your income tax forms are different. The real point of these precepts is to be the precepts. When you are the precepts, you realize that there is no giver and no receiver, and that there is nothing to give and nothing to receive. Whether you have taken these precepts or not, whether or not you even intend to, you are free to use them. They have the capability to nourish and to heal. They are the life of a Buddha. My life and your life.

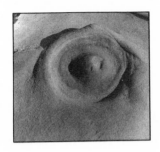

GLOSSARY

ANANDA The Buddha's disciple and personal attendant, known for having repeated all of the Buddha's discourses from memory at the First Council.

ANATMAN No-self; the *anatman* doctrine is one of the essential teachings of Buddhism, stating that there is no permanent, enduring substance within any entity; self is an idea.

ANUTTARA-SAMYAKSAMBODHI Supreme perfect enlightenment of a complete Buddha.

ASHOKA King of the Maurya kingdom in northern India from 272 to 236 B.C.E. He became a lay Buddhist follower and undertook the establishment of a "reign of dharma," causing Buddhism to gain a strong foothold in both India and Ceylon.

AVALOKITESHVARA The bodhisattva of compassion; "she who hears the outcries of the world"; also Kannon or Kanzeon.

BLUE CLIFF RECORD A collection of one hundred koans compiled, with appreciatory verses, by Master Hsüeh-tou Ch'ung-hsien (Jap. Setcho Juken), 982–1052, and with commentaries by Master Yüan-wu K'o-ch'in (Jap. Engo Kokugon), 1063–1135; a key text in the Rinzai Zen school, it was studied by Master Dogen, who carried a handwritten copy back to Japan from China.

BODHIDHARMA An Indian monk known for taking Buddhism from India to China and later Japan, where he settled at Shao-lin monastery and practiced zazen for nine years facing the wall; the "Barbarian from the West."

BODHI MIND Mind in which the aspiration for enlightenment has been awakened; the impulse that moves one toward self-realization.

BODHISATTVA One who practices the Buddha Way and compassionately postpones final enlightenment for the sake of others; the ideal of practice in Mahayana Buddhism.

BODHI TREE The fig tree under which the historical Buddha, Siddhartha Gautama, attained complete enlightenment.

BUDDHA-DHARMA Teachings of the Buddha based on his enlightenment experience; in Zen they are not to be conceptually understood but rather personally realized by each practitioner.

BUJI ZEN Free-styled, nonconformist attitude toward Zen training that arises out of an intellectual misunderstanding of Zen practice and enlightenment.

CHADO "The way of tea"; one of the Zen arts.

CHAO-CHOU (Jap. Joshu) One of the most important Zen masters of China during the Tang dynasty.

CHIH-I Founder of the T'ien-t'ai school of Chinese Buddhism.

COSMIC MUDRA Hand position used during zazen, also called the *dhyani*-mudra; the left hand rests on top of the right and the tips of the thumbs touch lightly; this gesture expresses seeing enlightenment within the world of appearances.

DANA PARAMITA Voluntary giving; considered in Buddhism as one of the most important virtues; one of the six paramitas, or perfections.

DENKAI Transmission of the precepts; one of the three aspects of the formal mind-to-mind transmission process between teacher and student.

DEVAS Divinities who inhabit the heavenly realm.

DHARANI A short sutra consisting of fundamental sounds that carry no extrinsic meaning.

DHARMA Universal truth or law; the Buddha's teachings; all phenomena that make up reality.

DHARMA COMBAT Unrehearsed dialogue in which two Zen practitioners test and sharpen their understanding of Zen truths.

DHARMAKAYA One of the three *kayas*, bodies of the Buddha; the body of the great order, essential reality; the unity of the Buddha and the existing universe.

DHARMA NAME Name given to a student by the teacher during jukai, the precepts ceremony.

DHYANA PARAMITA The perfection of meditation; the practice of using one's mind to cut through the illusion of an ego, and of experiencing oneself as not separate from other beings.

DIAMOND NET OF INDRA A description of the universe presented in the Flower Garland Sutra; it clearly displays the interconnections and interdependence of all the facets of reality through time and space.

DIAMOND SUTRA Key part of the Prajnaparamita collection of Buddha's teachings; it repeatedly reiterates that phenomenal appearances are illusory projections of the mind, empty of the self.

DOGEN ZENJI 1200–1253, founder of the Japanese Soto school of Zen; Dogen established Eihei-ji, the principal Soto training monastery in Japan; he is the author of the *Shobogenzo,* an important collection of dharma essays.

DOKUSAN/DAISAN Private interviews with the teacher during which students present and clarify their understanding of the dharma.

EIGHTFOLD PATH The content of the Buddha's fourth noble truth, the way out of suffering; it consists of right views, right determination, right speech, right action, right livelihood, right effort, right mindfulness, and right concentration.

EIGHT GATES OF TRAINING Training system used at Zen Mountain Monastery for complete living and realization; it includes zazen, Zen study with the teacher, academic study, liturgy, precepts practice, art practice, body practice, and work practice; it corresponds roughly to the aspects of the Buddha's Eightfold Path.

EISAI Dogen Zenji's first teacher; he was the first Japanese master to transmit the Zen tradition and the founder of the first Rinzai monastery.

ENLIGHTENMENT The direct experience of one's true nature.

"FAITH MIND SUTRA" A poem written by Chinese Zen master Seng-ts'an; it expounds Zen's basic spirit; famous for its opening sentence: "The Great Way is not difficult; it only avoids picking and choosing."

FIVE RANKS OF TUNG-SHAN A system of understanding existence's two components, the interplay of the absolute and the relative, developed by the Chinese Zen master Tung-shan Liang-chieh in the ninth century; it is also a formulation of different degrees of enlightenment.

FLOWER GARLAND SUTRA Mahayana sutra that constitutes the basis of the Chinese Hua-yen (Kegon) school; it emphasizes "mutually unobstructed interpenetration" and states that Buddha, mind, and universe are identical to one another.

FOUR NOBLE TRUTHS The first teaching of the historical Buddha; it addresses the nature of all suffering and points to the way of overcoming suffering; the truths are (1) life is suffering, (2) suffering has a cause, (3) there is an end to the cause of suffering, (4) the way to put an end to suffering is the Eightfold Path.

FOUR VOWS Vows taken by the bodhisattvas, expressing commitment to postpone their own enlightenment until all beings are liberated from delusion; they are chanted at the end of each day at Zen monasteries.

FUKANZAZENGI Dogen Zenji's "General Presentation of the Principles of Zazen," a fascicle stressing that zazen is not a means to enlightenment but is identical to it.

GARUDA BIRD A mythological being, half man, half bird, protector of Buddhist practice; occasionally used as a synonym for Buddha.

GASSHO Gesture of bringing one's hands together, palm to palm, embodying the identity of all dualities.

GATHA Short sutra that presents the dharma teachings in terse, pithy wording; frequently chanted.

GAUTAMA Shakyamuni; the historical Buddha.

GENJOKOAN: THE WAY OF EVERYDAY LIFE The first fascicle and the heart of Dogen Zenji's masterwork, *Shobogenzo*.

HARA Physical and spiritual center of one's body/mind; area in the lower belly used in centering one's attention in meditation and any activity.

HINAYANA "School of the Elders," or Theravada Buddhism, prevalent in the countries of southern Asia. It bases its teaching on the Four Noble Truths, the doctrine of dependent arising, and the concepts of karma and *anatman*.

HUI-K'O (JAP. EKA) The second Zen patriarch; in Zen lore, he cut off his arm and presented it to Bodhidharma to prove his earnestness as a student.

HUI-NENG (JAP. ENO) The sixth patriarch and author of the Platform Sutra, he is regarded as the father of the Zen tradition in China.

INO A monastic who is charged with the supervision and leading of ceremonies in a Zen monastery.

INTERDEPENDENT CO-ORIGINATION Doctrine that states that all psychological and physical phenomena constituting individual existence are interdependent and are relative to each other, and thus are ultimately unreal.

JUKAI Acknowledgment and reception of the Buddhist precepts; the ceremony of becoming a Buddhist.

KAI Precepts (Jap.)

KAISHI Preceptor; officiant giving the precepts during a jukai ceremony.

KALPA A world cycle; an endlessly long period of time.

KANNON See Avalokiteshvara.

KARMA The universal law of cause and effect, linking an action's underlying intention to that action's consequences; it equates the actions of body, speech, and thought as potential sources of karmic consequences.

KEIZAN ZENJI Founder of Soji-ji, one of the two principal monasteries of the Japanese Soto school, and author of the *Denko-roku* Transmission of the Light.

KENSHO "Seeing into one's own nature"; first experience of realization.

KESA Monk's outer robe, worn across one shoulder.

KLESHA "Trouble, defilement, passion"; refers to all the properties that dull the mind and actions, binding people to the cycle of rebirth.

KOAN An apparently paradoxical statement or question used in Zen training to induce in students an intense level of doubt, allowing them to cut through conventional and conditioned descriptions of reality and see directly into their true nature.

KOANS OF THE WAY OF REALITY A collection of 108 Zen koans, together with prologue, capping verse, and footnotes, culled from ancient and modern sources, that are particularly relevant to Zen practitioners today. It is part of koan study at Zen Mountain Monastery.

KSHANTI PARAMITA One of the six perfections; refers to the patience and tolerance that arise from the insight that all the problems of beings have causes.

LOTUS SUTRA Sutra that contains the essential teachings of the Mahayana school: the doctrines of the transcendental nature of the Buddha and of the possibility of universal liberation.

MAHAKASHYAPA The Buddha's first successor; he was renowned for his ascetic self-discipline and moral strictness.

MAHAYANA "Great Vehicle"; the Northern school of Buddhism that expresses and aims at the intrinsic connection between an individual's realization and the simultaneous enlightenment of all beings.

MANJUSHRI The bodhisattva of wisdom.

MARA Lord of the sixth heaven of the desire realm, he symbolizes the passions that overwhelm human beings and hinder their enlightenment.

MIND-TO-MIND TRANSMISSION Complete merging of the teacher and the student; the confirmation of a student's realization.

MONDO An informal, freewheeling dialogue between the teacher and the students that centers on some relevant aspect of the teachings.

MU One of the first koans used in koan training; the first case in Master Wu-men's *Gateless Gate* collection of koans.

MUDRA A bodily posture expressing a particular inner mind state.

MUSHIN An expression for detachment of mind, a state of complete naturalness and freedom from dualistic thinking and feeling.

MYOZEN RYONEN ZENJI Student and dharma succesor of Eisai and the second master of Dogen Zenji.

NAN-CH'ÜAN (JAP. NANSEN) Dharma succesor of Ma-tsu Tao-i and teacher to Chao-chou.

NIRMANAKAYA One of the three bodies of the Buddha; the earthly body and manifestation that a Buddha assumes to guide all sentient beings toward liberation.

NIRVANA Union with the absolute; in Zen it is essential to realize that samsara is nirvana, form is emptiness, that all beings are innately perfect from the outset.

ORISON A type of prayer in which the separation between supplicant and divinity disappears.

ORYOKI "Containing just enough"; the set of bowls used in a ceremonial meal eaten in silence in Buddhist monasteries, and the meal itself.

PARAMITAS Perfections; virtues of attitude and behavior cultivated by bodhisattvas in the course of their development, necessary on the path of transcendence or realization; "reaching the other shore"; the six paramitas are generosity, discipline, patience, exertion, meditation, and wisdom.

PLATFORM SUTRA Sutra containing the biography, discourses, and sayings of Master Hui-neng.

PRAJNA WISDOM Not that which is possessed but that which is directly and thoroughly experienced.

PRAJNAPARAMITA SUTRA Series of about forty Mahayana sutras dealing with the realization of prajna wisdom; they include the Diamond Sutra and the Heart Sutra, among others.

PRATYEKA-BUDDHA Term for one who has attained enlightenment on one's own and only for oneself. In the levels of sainthood, the *pratyeka-buddha* is placed between the arhats and the Buddhas.

PRECEPTS Moral and ethical guidelines that, in Buddhism, are a description of the life of a Buddha, one who realizes the nature of existence and acts out of that realization.

PRECEPTS KOANS 120 koans on the precepts taken by Mountains and Rivers Order Zen students prior to formal mind-to-mind transmission of the precepts.

PURE LAND BUDDHISTS Followers of a school of Chinese and Japanese Buddhism whose goal is to be reborn in the pure land of Amitabha by way of the recitation of his name, the *nembutsu*.

RAKUSU A small, more practical version of the kesa, "Buddha's robe"; a garment worn by Zen Buddhist practitioners across their chests.

RIGHT LIVELIHOOD One of the aspects of the Eightfold Path, it stresses the importance of avoiding professions that are harmful to sentient beings.

RINZAI SCHOOL School of Zen that originated with the great Chinese Zen master Lin-chi I-hsüan in the ninth century and was reformed by Master Hakuin in Japan; it stresses koan practice.

ROHATSU SESSHIN Sesshin done in Zen monasteries in commemoration of the Buddha's enlightenment. Traditionally run from the first to the eighth of December.

ROSHI "Old venerable master"; title of Zen teachers.

SAMADHI State in which the mind is absorbed in intense concentration, free from distractions and goals; the essential nature of the self can be experienced directly within samadhi.

SAMANTABHADRA Bodhisattva venerated as the protector of all those who teach the dharma, and regarded as the embodiment of insight into the unity of sameness and difference. Alternatively, the bodhisattva of perfect actions and conduct.

SAMBHOGAKAYA One of the three bodies of the Buddha; "body of bliss," or reward body.

SAMSARA Existence prior to liberation, conditioned by the three attitudes of greed, anger, and ignorance and marked by continuous rebirths.

SANGHA Community of practitioners; all sentient and insentient beings.

SATORI The experience of awakening; enlightenment.

SENG-TS'AN See Third Ancestor Seng-ts'an.

SESSHIN "Gathering of the mind"; an extended period of intensive meditation practice lasting between five and ten days, centered on zazen.

SHAKYAMUNI BUDDHA Siddhartha Gautama, the historical Buddha and the founder of Buddhism; he was a prince of the Shakya clan, living in northern India in the sixth century B.C.E.

SHIKANTAZA "Just sitting"; form of zazen in which one practices pure awareness.

SHILA Precepts; guidelines of enlightened conduct.

SHOBOGENZO "Treasury of the True Dharma Eye," a collection of writings and discourses of the Japanese master Dogen Zenji.

SHRAVAKAS Equivalent to arhats, they are students who seek personal enlightenment and can attain it only by listening to the teaching and gaining insight into the Four Noble Truths and the unreality of all phenomena.

SOTO SCHOOL One of the existing schools of Zen Buddhism, founded by the Chinese masters Tung-shan Liang-chieh and Ts'ao-shan Pen-chi in the ninth century; it was revitalized and brought to Japan by Dogen Zenji.

STUPA Memorial monument over the mortal remains of the historical Buddha and other saints.

SUCHNESS *Tathata;* the absolute, true state of phenomena. It is immutable, immovable, and beyond all concepts and distinctions.

SUNYATA Void; central principle of Buddhism that recognizes the emptiness of all composite entities, without reifying nothingness; resolution of all dualities.

SUTRA Narrative text consisting chiefly of the discourses and teachings of the Buddha.

TANTRA Tradition strongly oriented toward human's experiential potential, it describes spiritual development in terms of ground, path, and fruition.

TATHAGATA One of the titles of the Buddha, "thus-come one," referring to one who has attained the perfect enlightenment.

TEISHO Dharma discourse; a formal talk on a koan or on significant aspects of Zen teachings; not an intellectual presentation or a philosophical explanation but a teacher's direct expression of the spirit of Zen.

TENDAI BUDDHISM School based on the Lotus Sutra and the teaching of the three truths: emptiness, temporal limitation of existence, and suchness.

TEN OX-HERDING PICTURES An ancient Chinese descriptive device; a collection of drawings with accompanying comments and poems that presents the progress of a person on the path of self-realization.

TEN STAGES A schematic system delineating progressive phases of Zen training at Zen Mountain Monastery, based on the Ten Ox-Herding Pictures of Master K'uo-an.

THERAVADIN Pertaining to the Theravada, or Hinayana, school of Buddhism.

THIRD ANCESTOR SENG-TS'AN Dharma succesor of Hui-k'o and author of the Faith Mind Sutra.

THREE POISONS Greed, anger, and ignorance; characteristics of human existence that arise out of the deluded view of the universe.

THREE TREASURES Buddha, Dharma, and Sangha; respectively, one who is awakened, the true teachings, and the group of people living in accord with the teachings. The Three Treasures are also known as the places of refuge for Buddhist practitioners.

UPAYA Skillful means; forms that the teachings take, reflecting their appropriateness to the circumstances in which they appear.

VAIROCHANA BUDDHA One of the five transcendent Buddhas, associated with Samantabhadra Bodhisattva and often depicted making the gesture of supreme wisdom.

VERSE OF THE KESA Short sutra chanted after the morning meditation period, expressing one's identification with the teachings of the Buddha.

VINAYA School of Buddhism that centers its practice on strict and precise observance of monastic rules and ethical precepts; collection of Buddhist precepts.

YASUTANI ROSHI One of the first Zen masters to be active in the West, he was succesor to Sogaku Harada and teacher to Koun Yamada Roshi. He was trained in both the Soto and Rinzai schools of Zen.

ZAZEN Sitting meditation, taught in Zen as the most direct way to enlightenment; the practice of the realization of one's own true nature.

ZENDO Meditation hall.

About Zen Mountain Monastery

Zen Mountain Monastery is an American Zen Buddhist monastery and training center for monastics and lay practitioners. It is located on a 230-acre site on Tremper Mountain in New York's Catskill Mountains, surrounded by state forest wilderness and featuring an environmental studies area. The Monastery provides a year-round daily training program that includes Zen meditation, various forms of face-to-face teaching, academic studies, liturgy, work practice, body practice, art practice, and study of the Buddhist Precepts. Each month a weekend introductory Zen training workshop, and a week-long silent Zen meditation retreat (sesshin) are offered. During the spring and fall quarters of each year, ninety-day intensive programs (Angos) are conducted. Throughout the year, the regular daily schedule is supplemented with seminars and workshops in the Zen arts, the martial arts, Buddhist studies, and other areas relevant to present-day Western practitioners. Students can train in either full-time or part-time residency or as non-residents whose "home practice" is fueled by periodic visits to the Monastery. For further information, contact:

Registrar
Zen Mountain Monastery
P.O. Box 197
Mount Tremper, NY 12457
(914) 688-2228
Home Page Address: http://www1.mhv.net/~dharmacom
E-mail: dharmacom@mhv.net

294.3
LOO

Loori, John Daido.

The heart of being.

$16.95